HIGHER MODERN STU

UK Social Issues

Frank Cooney, Irene Morrison
& George Clarke

HODDER
GIBSON
AN HACHETTE UK COMPANY

The Publishers would like to thank the following for permission to reproduce copyright material:

Photo credits
p.1 (l) © nyul – Fotolia, (r) © Lisa F. Young – Fotolia; p.5 © Ethel Davis / Robert Harding / Rex Features; p.7 © Hulton Archive / Getty Images; p.8 © Dan Kitwood / Staff / Getty Images; p.10 © Christopher Furlong/Staff / Getty Images; p.14 © Yakoniva / Alamy; p.17 © Daniel Atkin / Alamy; p.18 © Giles Moberly / PYMCA / Rex Features; p.20 © Bubbles Photolibrary / Alamy; p.23 © ACE STOCK LIMITED / Alamy; p.25 © John McKenna / Alamy; p.26 © All rights reserved by alpha deux cents (http://www.flickr.com/photos/seritiku/); p.29 © Steve Bell / Rex Features; p.30 © adrian arbib / Alamy; p.32 © Nils Jorgensen / Rex Features; p.34 © Lydia Austin; p.37 © Bruce Adams / Associated Newspapers / Rex Features; p.39 © Oli Scarff / Staff / Getty Images; p.41 © Richard Gardner / Rex Features; p.46 © Ian Dagnall / Alamy; p.47 (both) © Mike Bolam Photography; p.50 (tl) © David Robertson / Alamy, (tr) © Tom Plesnik / Fotolia.com, (b) © Paul Thompson / Corbis; p.53 © Monkey Business / Fotolia.com; p.56 © Dinodia Photos / Alamy; p.63 (t) © diego cervo – Fotolia, (b) © Getty Images; p.66 © Marco Secchi / Alamy; p.69 © Wojciech Gajda – Fotolia; p.71 © Rex Features; p.73 © Duncan Hale-Sutton / Alamy; p.77 © Esther Hildebrandt – Fotolia; p.80 © Martin Barraud; p.81 © Rex Features; p.83 © Daniel Atkin / Alamy; p.87 © Ted Foxx / Alamy; p.88 © Peter Dazeley; p.91 © Blake-Ezra Cole / Rex Features; p.93 © Kaliani Lyle / Equality and Human Rights Commission; p.95 © Rex Features.

Chapter opener image reproduced on pages 1, 7, 15, 28, 44, 59 and 75 © c / Fotolia.com.

Acknowledgements
Extract on page 80 from 'Female doctors fail to break through the glass ceiling' by Rachel Ellis, published in *The Observer* on 22 August 2010 Copyright Guardian News & Media Ltd 2010.

Every effort has been made to trace all copyright holders, but if any have been inadvertently overlooked the Publishers will be pleased to make the necessary arrangements at the first opportunity.

Orders: please contact Bookpoint Ltd, 130 Milton Park, Abingdon, Oxon OX14 4SB. Telephone: (44) 01235 827720. Fax: (44) 01235 400454. Lines are open 9.00–5.00, Monday to Saturday, with a 24-hour message answering service. Visit our website at www.hoddereducation.co.uk. Hodder Gibson can be contacted direct on: Tel: 0141 848 1609; Fax: 0141 889 6315; email: hoddergibson@hodder.co.uk

© Frank Cooney, Irene Morrison and George Clarke 2011
First published in 2011 by
Hodder Gibson, an imprint of Hodder Education,
An Hachette UK Company
2a Christie Street
Paisley PA1 1NB

Impression number 5 4 3 2 1
Year   2014 2013 2012 2011

Cover photo (top) © Robin Weaver / Alamy, (bottom) © Digital Vision / Getty Images
Illustrations by Fakenham Prepress Solutions and Jeff Edwards
Typeset in Minion Pro 12pt by Fakenham Prepress Solutions, Fakenham, Norfolk NR21 8NN
Printed in Italy

A catalogue record for this title is available from the British Library

ISBN: 978 1444 137088

Contents

Social Class in Britain

Social class involves factors such as wealth, income and occupation as well as status, lifestyle, values, beliefs, levels of education, etc. We are all aware that members of the royal family are upper class and that Prince William married a commoner in April 2011. Social class can influence our future prosperity and even impact on our future health. (This is discussed in Chapters 2–5.) Social class is very complex. To make it more manageable, occupation has been used to measure social class.

The Registrar General's Model of Social Class (RGSC) was used by UK governments from 1911 to 1980. Society was divided into six categories according to occupation. Occupations were ranked by 'their standing in the community' relative to each other.

A   Professional occupations

B   Managerial and technical occupations

Figure 1.1 A white-collar worker ↑

C1   Non-manual skilled occupations

C2   Manual skilled occupations

Figure 1.2 A manual worker ↑

D   Partly skilled occupations

E   Unskilled occupations

The model was simple to understand and apply and it enabled government statisticians to compare health between different groups, provide analysis of employment and unemployment, and investigate poverty and family life across time. The results enabled governments to target resources for social planning.

However, because it used a person's occupation to classify them, the model omitted large sections of the population, such as those who were retired and the unemployed. It also left out wives or husbands who were unemployed and those groups whose incomes came from rents or investments. Another problem was that the categories were too broad, for example a farmer could be a poor smallholder or a millionaire gentleman farmer. (Nevertheless, this model of social class is still important today because it is still used by many organisations in, for example, analysing how people vote and to measure their health and wellbeing.) Health statistics tend to use numbers rather than letters, for example 1 is Social class A and 5 is Social Class E.

In response to these shortcomings, government statisticians introduced a new model called the Standard Occupation Classification (SOC) in 1980. It replaced the RGSC and lasted until 2001. It had nine major categories and these were further subdivided.

In 2001, the Office for National Statistics (ONS) introduced the National Statistics Socio-economic Classification (NS-SeC), which it uses for all official statistics and surveys. The NS-SeC is based on occupation but is designed to provide coverage of the whole adult population (see Table 1.1).

Sociologists use other ways of measuring social class, for example Hutton's 30/30/40 Society and the Runciman Scale.

Hutton says that the economies of modern industrial societies have created a labour

Table 1.1 **The National Statistics Socio-economic Classification**

	Classification		**Description**
1	Higher managerial and professional occupations		
	1.1	Large employers and higher managerial occupations	company directors, senior managers, senior civil servants, senior police officers
	1.2	Higher professional occupations	doctors, lawyers, teachers and social workers
2	Lower managerial and professional occupations		nurses, journalists, actors, musicians, lower ranks in the police and armed forces
3	Intermediate occupations		clerks, secretaries, driving instructors, telephone fitters
4	Small employers and own account workers		publicans, farmers, window cleaners, painters and decorators
5	Lower supervisory and technical occupations		printers, plumbers, TV engineers, butchers
6	Semi-routine occupations		shop assistants, hairdressers, bus drivers, cooks
7	Routine occupations		couriers, labourers, waiters, refuse collectors
8	Never worked and long-term unemployed		non-working spouses, unemployed for various reasons
	'Not classified' is added to cover students and other groups		

Source: Office for National Statistics

market that divides people into three categories. There are the advantaged who are in full-time, well-paid and secure employment. At the bottom are the disadvantaged who suffer unemployment and are excluded. Between the two is a group whose employment is insecure and who are striving to become advantaged but are more likely to become disadvantaged.

The Runciman Scale is based around economic power, ownership, control and status based on a person's marketability. If a person owns a company, they have economic power. If a person has the power to direct others in the workplace, they have economic power. If a person possesses skills that are prized by society, they have economic power. Therefore a person's social class is based on the extent of economic power they have either through the things they own or the skills they possess.

Activities

1 Why does defining social class still matter?

2 What factors can determine social class?

3 Note the main models used to define social class with a brief explanation for each.

Does class exist in the twenty-first century?

The economy of the UK went through radical change during the twentieth century. This had a major impact on social class.

The number of manual workers fell from three-quarters of the working population to just over one-third. This was matched by the growth of the AB groups (managers, professionals, etc.) from 15 per cent in 1911 to nearly 40 per cent by the end of the century. Numbers of clerical workers and sales workers also increased significantly.

The UK continues to have an upwardly mobile class structure but it is slowing down because there are fewer and fewer children whose parents are in lower class groups, so fewer people can move upwards.

Another significant change in social class is the number of women who are counted as part of the workforce. In 1900, there were 5 million women workers who accounted for only 29 per cent of the workforce. Therefore most women in the UK were placed in a social class group dependent on their husband's status. A century later the number of women workers had increased to 13 million and accounted for 46 per cent of the total workforce and are categorised in their own right.

In a 2005 study, *Moving Up and Down the Social Class Ladder in Scotland* by Cristina Iannelli and Lindsay Paterson, the researchers found that nearly two-thirds of adults of working age had moved to a different social class to that in which they were brought up, and more than two-thirds of these had moved up the social class ladder.

They also found that there was a reduction in upward mobility compared with earlier generations. There were fewer people born into manual class groups because these groups had contracted. So there are fewer people able to move up. There is some upward mobility and some people do drift downwards but the overwhelming majority remain within the social group they are born into.

A 2011 report by The Prince's Trust Scotland confirms the above findings. Almost 19 per cent of young people from Scotland's poorest families believe they will achieve few or none of their goals in life and they expect 'to end up in a dead-end job'. Geraldine Gemmell, Director of The Prince's Trust Scotland, stated, 'the aspiration gap between Scotland's richest and poorest young people was creating a youth underclass'.

Therefore in the twenty-first century social class divisions are far less clear and much less rigid than they were even 50 years ago. However, the evidence indicates that wide variations remain in terms of living standards, the quality of life and life chances in people born into different classes.

In the recent past, the income, wealth and living standards of people in higher occupational classes have increased faster than those in the lower occupational classes. For example, a child born in the poorest constituency in Scotland is three times more likely to be born into a workless household and depend on benefits, and twice as likely to have no qualifications and to live 15 years less than a child born into a less poor constituency. Children of unskilled manual labourers suffer more ill health than the children of professional parents. They are four times more likely to die in an accident. Their health is generally worse, they are more likely to be obese and their infant mortality rates are higher.

This is reflected in the geographic spread of wealth, health and poverty in the UK. The North–South divide clearly exists and is discussed in later chapters.

Children born into higher social classes do better in education and have a better chance of getting higher-paid jobs. For example, most children of unskilled workers become unskilled workers and most children of professional workers become professional workers themselves. Therefore it is clear that social class exists and impacts on our life chances.

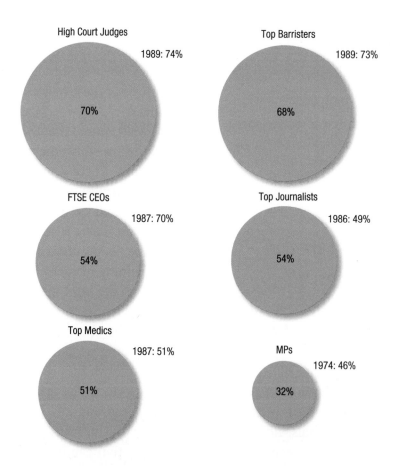

Figure 1.3 Britain's low level of social mobility: How top occupations are dominated by the privately educated (7 per cent of the population are privately educated). Encircled figures are correct for 2010 ↑

The return of the Conservatives to power in their coalition with the Liberal Democrats has once again opened the debate that the UK is becoming a less classless society. The top posts in society are dominated by those who attended private schools, for example 70 per cent of judges went to private schools (see Figure 1.3). The 2011 Cabinet reflects the dominance of wealth and private education.

A *Sunday Times* article in May 2010 had the headline 'Cutback Cabinet has 18 millionaires' (there are 23 ministers in the Cabinet). Top of the list is Philip Hammond, the Transport Secretary, with an estimated fortune of £7.1 million. In third place is the Chancellor, George Osborne, with an estimated fortune of £4.6 millon. As Osborne slashes public expenditure it is difficult to accept David Cameron's view that 'We are all in this together.'

In a 2010 BBC programme titled *Posh and Posher: Why public schoolboys run Britain,* journalist and media personality Andrew Neil argued that political meritocracy has now ended and that the political elite are all privately educated. His evidence is persuasive: Cameron and Clegg went to the top public schools and of the 119 ministers in the government 10 per cent went to Eton and 66 per cent were privately educated. Labour also has become more elitist – a third of the Shadow Cabinet attended either Oxford or Cambridge.

To the extent it is possible to arrange the population into identifiable groups with measurable differences it is reasonable to say that social class continues to exist in the twenty-first century and that social mobility is less evident.

Figure 1.4 School students entering Eton ↑

Absolute poverty and relative poverty

The United Nations says absolute poverty is 'a condition characterised by severe deprivation of basic human needs'. It lists basic human needs as food, safe drinking water, sanitation facilities, health, shelter, education and access to benefits. A person is said to be living in absolute poverty *only* if he or she is deprived of two or more of these seven basic human needs.

Relative poverty compares the living standards of people in the lowest sections of a population with those in the upper levels. Measuring relative poverty is largely the same as measuring inequality. Therefore as the distribution of income changes in a society, then the scale of relative poverty will be altered. If a society gets a more equal income distribution, relative poverty will fall.

How do we measure poverty in the UK?

The main government measure is provided by the Department of Work and Pensions (DWP) in its annual report on Households Below Average Income (HBAI). The HBAI report identifies poverty as 60 per cent of the median income. (Median income is the middle income in a range of all incomes in the UK. It is the income that has 50 per cent of the nation's incomes above it and 50 per cent below it.)

A second method is to use Income Support levels. These are set by Parliament to provide a basic income for people between the ages of 16 and 60 who are living on a low income because they are incapable of work due to illness or disability, or they care for a sick or disabled person, or they are a lone parent responsible for a child under 16. Income Support is means tested. Regulations approved by Parliament state the levels of income appropriate to various circumstances, for example age, family size, disabilities, before an award is made.

As Income Support levels are set to reflect the income required to meet basic needs they can be used as a measure of poverty. However, they are set as the consequence of a political agenda so may not accurately reflect poverty levels in the UK, as political considerations will influence the levels set.

Finally, the *Poverty and Social Exclusion* (PSE) survey provides an alternative measure. (This is discussed in Chapter 3.) These three measures of poverty measure different things. The HBAI survey is a statistical calculation based on the range of incomes that exist in the UK at a point in time. The Income Support calculation is intended to identify a basic level of income necessary to survive in the UK but is influenced by political considerations. Finally, the PSE survey measures the level of poverty among various sections of society by using a snapshot of the public's perceptions of what things are necessary for life in modern Britain. It is a measure of the public's perception of poverty.

Activities

1 What factors have caused a reduction in social class divisions in the last 50 years?

2 What evidence is there to support the view that social class still exists in the UK today and that products of public schools are the political and social elite?

3 It may be argued that very few people in the UK live in absolute poverty but relative poverty affects a significant number. Explain this point of view.

4 Design a diagram or table to help you remember the three main methods used to measure poverty in the UK.

5 Why do you think we should not rely on just one of these models when explaining levels of poverty?

2 The Welfare State

The founding principles of the Welfare State

When the Beveridge Report was published in 1942, its recommendations amounted to a comprehensive attack on what Beveridge called the 'five giants standing in the way of social progress', namely Want, Disease, Ignorance, Squalor and Idleness. The report dealt only with the first of these 'giants', Want – what we would now call poverty. Beveridge argued, however, that if people were to be kept out of poverty it would also be necessary for the other four 'giants' to be tackled.

The new national health system introduced in 1948 would make the population healthier, which would improve the productive resources of the country and reduce the costs of Social Security. Moreover, Beveridge expected that the costs to the state of providing this health care would, through time, decline, or at least remain stable, as the backlog of those suffering from ill health was eliminated.

Beveridge's five giants

- **Eliminating Want** – by reforming and extending the social security system.
- **Eliminating Disease** – by the creation of a new national health service.
- **Eliminating Ignorance** – by the introduction of educational reforms.
- **Eliminating Squalor** – by a programme to improve living conditions, in particular to provide adequate housing.
- **Eliminating Idleness** – by the promotion of economic policies that would ensure high and stable levels of employment.

The Welfare State was based on four principles. It was to be collectivist, universal, comprehensive and equal. The post-war Labour Government's legacy was to introduce a welfare system and

Figure 2.1 William Beveridge ↑

a national health service that made the state responsible for providing financial support for those without adequate income, health care, education and decent housing, and help in finding employment. It would provide a service 'from the cradle to the grave'.

Collectivist

The state would fund the services needed.

The Government raised funds through National Insurance contributions and general taxation. It also took responsibility for directing policy. The Treasury decided the levels of pensions and benefits and succeeding governments decided on the levels of investment in the National Health Service (NHS), then through local authorities it decided how much was to be spent on social housing and education.

However, the rising costs involved in these services have made successive governments review the way the Welfare State was funded. People on the right of the political spectrum argue that the enormous sums spent on the Welfare State undermine economic growth because of the levels of taxation it needs. Some suggest that benefit levels force wage levels up and make UK production uncompetitive. They also argue that welfare reduces incentives to encourage individuals to find their own solutions to their problems. For example, benefits allow the unemployed to avoid seeking work or taking low-paid employment. Health provision stops individuals providing private health care for themselves.

Those on the left criticise the Welfare State for not giving enough help to important groups in our society, such as women and ethnic minorities.

Increasingly, aspects of public welfare have been devolved away from direct government funding. In social housing, the Thatcher Government in the 1980s sold off large numbers of council houses to private buyers while more recently the management of the social housing that remains has been handed over to housing associations, for example in Glasgow. In education and the health service, new schools and hospitals were funded by the private finance initiative. In higher education, students will have to pay annual tuition fees of up to £9000 in England and Wales. In Scotland, graduates have to repay loans when their salaries reach a certain level.

David Cameron's Big Society aims to provide greater choice in schools, health and community services. However, this provision should be organised and run by charities and volunteers as an alternative to what the Conservative Government sees as the big state (see Cameron's Big Society on page 10).

Therefore the welfare system is only partly collectivist.

Universal

The second aim of the Welfare State was to provide a range of services for the whole population that was free at the point of need.

However, from the beginning the universal principle was not applied across all provisions. Although universal health care has remained

Figure 2.2 Students demonstrating against higher university tuition fees in England and Wales ↑

largely free at the point of need, there have been charges made for prescriptions, dental care and eye treatment (see Paying for health – the options on page 11). Free compulsory education up to the age of 16 remains a universal provision. However, the provision of places in higher education has now given way to the introduction of tuition fees in England and Wales.

Even from the beginning the idea of basing entitlements on National Insurance contributions meant that many people – mainly women – were excluded and had to depend on means-tested benefits. The Labour Government 1997 to 2010 had a policy approach that it called 'progressive universalism'. This was the extension of means testing. So benefits they introduced, such as Pension Credit and Working Tax Credit, were means tested. Child Benefit was to be paid to the parents of all children irrespective of income. Labour retained Child Benefit as a universal benefit as a recognition of the extra cost of bringing up children. However, in 2013 the Coalition Government will end Child Benefit payments to higher-rate taxpayers, which means Child Benefit will be means tested rather than universal.

Therefore the Welfare State is not universal across the range of services.

Comprehensive

The state would undertake to provide for all aspects of need.

As stated, Beveridge wanted a welfare state to 'slay the five giants of want, disease, ignorance, squalor and idleness'. The extent to which the Welfare State has tackled each of these problems varies.

For example, the creation of the NHS meant a commitment to provide 'a comprehensive health service for the improvement of the physical and mental health of the people … for the prevention, diagnosis and treatment of illness'. Therefore the NHS was taking on the responsibility for all aspects of the nation's health care. To a great extent the NHS has provided an increasing level of prevention and treatment. However, as specialist consultants vary from area to area and some drugs are available in some areas and not in others – the postcode lottery – every person does not have access to all treatments in all areas of the UK. Therefore there are geographic inequalities in the NHS (see Chapters 5 and 6).

To tackle squalor, affordable council house accommodation was to be available in all areas. However, the 'Right to Buy' scheme introduced by the Conservative Government in the 1980s led to thousands of the best houses being sold off at discounted prices. Subsequently, insufficient quantities of social housing have been built. In 2010 in Scotland alone, 5500 houses were built by housing associations and 343 by councils while more than 160,000 households were on waiting lists. The ability of the state to provide social housing has deteriorated.

The attempts by the state to tackle poverty and unemployment have met with varying degrees of success depending on the economy of the country. In the last three years, with the economy having problems, both poverty and unemployment are increasing despite a variety of programmes to tackle them (see Chapters 3 and 4).

Therefore the Welfare State is not as comprehensive as Beveridge intended.

Equality

The aim of the Welfare State was for equal provision for all people in all regions and areas.

Yet in the NHS, to take one example, there has always been inequality. From the beginning, private health care provided more opportunities for those who were wealthy. In some areas the provision was better than others. For example, an

Cameron's Big Society

Most governments define their difference from previous governments by having a 'big idea'. Tony Blair's was 'The Third Way', which involved merging the best of socialist principles, for example the national minimum wage with market principles such as private sector involvement in the NHS. 'The Big Society', developed by Cameron when he was in opposition, is based on the view that 'the British state has become too big, impersonal and monolithic'. Cameron wishes to reduce the power of central government and for local communities to take greater responsibility in running worthwhile local services such as parks and libraries. His government's inclusive slogan 'We're all in this together' is being smothered by accusations that this project is a cynical cover for public sector cuts.

Cameron's new caring conservatism is being undermined by local government cuts. Local councils are reducing their own grants to voluntary organisations that help the homeless and the disabled. Some local councils, such as Fulham, are selling off buildings used by voluntary organisations. Other local councils, such as Northumberland, have entered ground-renting contracts with private for-profit recycling clothes companies to replace the clothes banks of voluntary organisations such as the British Heart Foundation. From this Northumberland council will receive about £200,000 in fees. There are more than 8000 charity shops in the UK and therefore donations to clothing banks on local government property is an important source of income.

area where there was a teaching hospital would have more experienced specialists and could provide more treatments. The postcode lottery means that some treatments are available to some people in some areas and not to others. Waiting lists have always been a way of rationing care and these have varied in length from area to area.

Rationing of health spending is also used. In May 2011 Mr Devine, a 68-year-old Scottish patient with a rare blood disorder, was denied a life-transforming drug on the grounds of cost by NHS Greater Glasgow and Clyde. Other health boards provide this drug, eculizumab, to patients. Mr Devine died shortly after this refusal.

Therefore welfare is not provided equally in all regions and all areas.

Figure 2.3 David Cameron ↑

Paying for health – the options

The Coalition Government and the SNP Government have both stated that health spending will increase. However, the increase is below the rate of inflation and after years of growth cuts will have to be made. This has once again opened up the debate of funding the NHS.

● Raise taxes

Advantages: Easy to operate and allows swift access to funds. Opinion polls suggest that voters would favour an increase in taxation to provide greater funds for health and education.

Disadvantages: Politically risky. Historically the Labour Party has been regarded as a party of high taxation and views such a tag as a vote loser.

● Levy a specific (hypothecated) health care tax

Advantages: Public would be able to see where their money is being spent and may be less resistant to paying more.

Revenue raised from smokers could, for example, be additional income awarded to the NHS.

Disadvantages: Additional costs of raising or administering the money may not result in proportionate benefits; could undermine willingness to fund less popular spending. Politically a risky move.

● Introduce compulsory state approved insurance (stakeholder health insurance)

Advantages: Provides general cover, yet gives consumers more indication of what they are paying for. Proposal could be extended to enable poorer people to have their premiums paid for by the Government.

Disadvantages: Problems for those who are not in employment and cannot afford health cover; an additional financial burden; could be regarded as an increase in taxation. If extended to all adults a means-tested system would have to be introduced.

● Encourage more private health insurance

Advantages: People can choose to pay for what they want; adds to health care without increasing taxation.

Disadvantages: No access to treatment for the poor and those considered 'high risk'; administration can be expensive; may divert resources from NHS. Tax relief on medical insurance premiums will reduce government income.

● Apply user charges

Advantages: Raises ready money – £5 per GP visit could raise £1 billion; £10 a day for hospital accommodation could raise £200 million.

Disadvantages: Would be unpopular with the public and destroy the concept of a 'free' NHS. There would have to be exemptions for the young, the elderly and the poor and an expensive bureaucracy would have to be set up to administer the scheme. It would create discord in hospitals with those patients paying 'hotel charges' expecting preferential treatment and service.

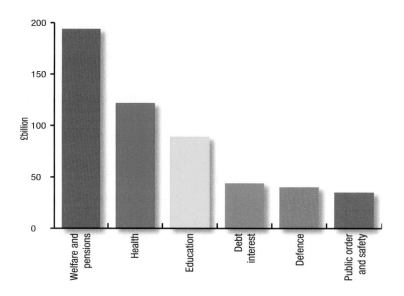

Figure 2.4 Cost of the Welfare State: Government spending, biggest items, £billion 2010–11 ↑

Source: June Budget forecast, 2010

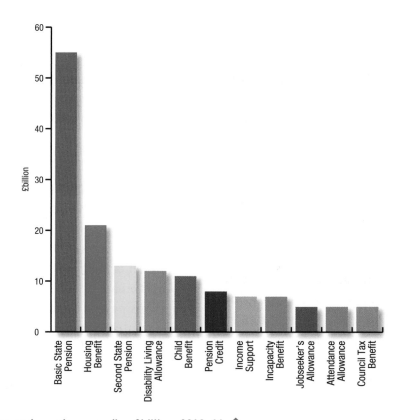

Figure 2.5 Key welfare and pension spending £billion, 2010–11 ↑

Source: DWP Forecast (*Sunday Times*, 3 October 2010)

The funding of the Welfare State

Figures 2.4 and 2.5 highlight that welfare spending takes up a significant amount of government spending. The annual repayment of the debt alone is £44 billion. The massive spending cuts of 2010–15 (£81 billion) to reduce the budget deficit will impact on all our lives, whether employed or unemployed. Welfare spending will take its share of the cuts. The impact of these cuts is discussed in Chapter 4.

NHS workforce and budget

Health spending in Scotland reached a record level of £11.3 billion in 2011–12, a third of the total Scottish budget, reflecting the massive cash injection of the Labour Governments. Based on population, Scotland employs 30 per cent more health staff than does England – 10,000 extra NHS staff have been employed over the last ten years. (The Scottish workforce is 169,000 and UK workforce is 1.3 million.) The Scottish Government will need to reduce public spending by about 11 per cent in the period 2011–15 but has pledged to increase NHS spending by about 1 per cent a year. Unfortunately, the increase in the number of elderly people and the cost of new medicines and technologies requires an annual 5 per cent increase to maintain its present services so the NHS will experience real-term cuts – under efficiency savings around 4000 posts disappeared in 2010–11. The NHS is a victim of its own success as new expensive technology and medicines enable individuals to live longer, thus placing further pressure on the NHS.

The elderly

The elderly is a growing group within society: in the 1970s anyone who reached the age of 60 could expect to live another 18 years; in 2010 this has risen to 28 years. However, there are significant geographic differences in UK life expectancy (see Table 2.1). This places significant demands on the NHS and pension provision. Some critics argue that the elderly suffer from health inequalities in terms of ageism within the NHS and a failure to provide sufficient funding to care for their health needs. Numerous reports have highlighted the poor treatment that many elderly people receive in hospitals or care homes. A 2008 report by the Healthcare Commission Inspectorate stated that 'the elderly are being neglected, treated poorly and marginalised in the healthy system'.

Table 2.1 **The highest and lowest life expectancies in the UK by selected local authorities**

Men	Age expectancy
Kensington and Chelsea	84.4
Westminster	83.4
Epsom and Ewell	81.8
Inverclyde	73.1
West Dunbartonshire	72.5
Glasgow City	71.1
Women	**Age expectancy**
Kensington and Chelsea	89.0
Westminster	86.5
Hart	85.6
North Lanarkshire	78.5
West Dunbartonshire	78.4
Glasgow City	77.5

Source: UK Government Health Statistics, 2010

Figure 2.6 An elderly person in a care home ↑

The Sutherland report of 1999 recommended that medical care in nursing and residential homes should be provided free and should not be means tested. The UK Government refused to implement its findings on the grounds of cost. In contrast the Scottish Executive introduced free personal care for the elderly and regards it as one of its flagship policies.

In England pensioners living in care homes can receive Social Security payments (nursing care and attendance allowances) that are means tested and paid from the UK Social Security budget. These funds are no longer available to Scottish recipients of personal care. This means that the cost of free personal care is totally paid by the Scottish taxpayer with the Scottish Executive no longer able to access the UK budget.

In 2010 Lord Sutherland, the architect of Scotland's free elderly care, admitted that the policy should be reviewed given the massive pressure on public funding. The cost has more than doubled from £129 million in 2004 to £274 million today. It is clear that with our ageing population the cost of free personal care will continue to increase significantly.

Activities

1 Design a diagram to help you remember the four founding principles of the Welfare State.

2 Why might it be argued that the Welfare State in the UK has never lived up to these principles?

3 Explain the individualist approach to welfare. Give some examples of government policies that followed this approach.

4 Explain the collectivist approach to welfare. Give some examples of government policies that followed this approach.

5 Describe Cameron's Big Society idea and why it has been criticised.

6 Refer to Figures 2.4 and 2.5. Why do welfare and pensions take up so much of the budget?

7 Why is the NHS a victim of its own success?

Inequalities in Wealth

The *Poverty and Social Exclusion in the United Kingdom* (*PSE*) survey is a major research project funded by the Economic and Social Research Council (ESRC) that was launched in May 2010 and will be completed in 2013. The project is investigating the best ways to measure poverty, deprivation, social exclusion and standards of living, what the current extent and nature of poverty is and what policies best address these problems. This research will repeat the 1999 survey funded by the Joseph Rowntree Foundation (JRF). The findings of the research will hopefully help us understand more about what causes poverty and what the most effective strategies might be to deal with the problem.

Deprivation and poverty

Measures of deprivation relate to how people live and are not the same as measures of income. Deprivation is the consequence of a lack of income and other resources that cumulatively can be seen as living in poverty. This approach to poverty looks at indicators of deprivation and then relates them to income levels. Peter Townsend, in 1968–69, developed a list of 60 indicators of the population's 'style of living' into standards of living in the UK. The indicators included the following: diet, clothing, fuel and lighting, home amenities, immediate environment of the home, security of work, family support, recreation, education, health and social relations. A lack or non-participation in these was seen as an indicator of deprivation.

This could then be related to household income and hence to a level of poverty. Critics of this approach argue that the indicators of deprivation were arbitrary and that they failed to allow for difference and choice in how people lived.

Wealth and poverty across Britain

The Joseph Rowntree Foundation Survey

JRF carried out a study into Britain's wealth and poverty distribution from 1968 to 2005. The key findings of that research included:

- Britain has moved back towards levels of inequality in wealth and poverty that existed more than 40 years ago.

- There is less extreme poverty but there has been an increase in households where people live just below the standard poverty line – JRF call these the 'breadline poor'. In parts of some cities, more than half of all households are 'breadline poor'.

- There is evidence that rich and poor now live further apart. Urban clustering of poverty has risen while the wealthier households concentrate in the outskirts of major cities, especially London. The Rich List for 2010 (*Sunday Times*) stated that the top 1000 multi-millionaires in the UK saw their wealth increase between

2009 and 2010 by 30 per cent – the largest percentage increase year on year in the 22 years of The Rich List – and at a time when the UK and most of the rest of the world economy was going through its worst economic crisis since the Great Depression.

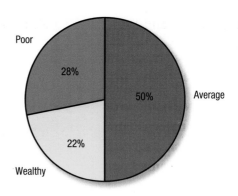

Figure 3.1 Distribution of households in 2007 ↑

British Social Attitudes Survey 2010

The British Social Attitudes Survey 2010 showed that nearly 8 in 10 people think the gap between those on high and low incomes is too large. Around 63 per cent think that income inequality leads to social problems like crime. The survey also highlighted that there is much support for ensuring more equality of opportunity as well as a view that taxes are too high for people on low incomes. The survey also asked its 3000 respondents about how this inequality might be reduced (this is discussed in Chapter 4). Three main ways were identified:

- 62 per cent supported the idea that better education or training opportunities should be provided to enable people to get better jobs.
- 56 per cent said that people on lower incomes should pay less tax and that those on higher incomes should pay more.
- 54 per cent said the minimum wage should be increased (see pages 29–32).

Overall, people in Britain do not believe there is equal opportunity in Britain today. They believe that the more unequal a society is the greater the range of social problems, such as mental health issues, high obesity, morbidity and mortality rates, higher rates of incarceration, violence, teenage pregnancy.

Poverty is not just about income or material wellbeing but is also about wellbeing in other senses. It is about the wider dimensions of poverty, for example poor health, poor education, housing, environment and social opportunities.

Activities

1 Why are organisations such as the Joseph Rowntree Foundation important in our understanding of the problems associated with, for example, poverty?

2 Why might using income levels to determine poverty levels be a useful measurement?

3 Why might using deprivation measures to determine poverty levels be useful?

4 What evidence is there of poverty across the UK?

Groups vulnerable to poverty

Minority ethnic groups

This topic is covered in more depth in Chapter 7.

Evidence of poverty

The income poverty rate for minority ethnic groups is about 40 per cent compared to 20 per cent for White British people. There are big differences in poverty rates across the ethnic groups. Risks of income poverty are highest for Bangladeshis and Pakistanis but also above average for Indians and Chinese.

Table 3.1 **Income poverty rates vary greatly between the ethnic groups**

Minority ethnic group	Income poverty rate (%)
Bangladeshis	65
Pakistanis	55
Black Africans	45
Black Caribbeans	30
Indians	25
White British	20

For all ages, family types and work statuses, people from minority ethnic groups are, on average, more likely to be in income poverty than White British people. Almost 70 per cent of those in income poverty in inner London are from minority ethnic groups. Minority ethnic groups are being overlooked for jobs and are being paid lower wages.

Figure 3.2 A disadvantaged child ↑

Child poverty

Official measures of child poverty are based on national surveys of family income. In England, one child in five is classified as living in poverty. In some areas of large cities this rises to more than half, for example Tower Hamlets in London. In six London boroughs and in Manchester, at least four out of ten children are living in poverty. In the constituency of Bethnal Green and Bow in London the percentage of children living in poverty in 2010 was 57 per cent. Poverty has devastating effects on children. It affects their life. Growing up in poverty can affect every area

Case Study: Child poverty

Poverty shortens lives. A girl in Manchester can expect to live six years less than a girl in the Chelsea area of London. Living in poverty can have an impact on children from a very early age. For example, disadvantage in Dundee may start at birth. In the more deprived areas of the city, there is a high incidence of low weight babies and the ongoing effects of a poorer start in life. Low birth weight is closely associated with infant death and chronic diseases in later life. The risk of infant mortality is higher for poor children. In the lower social group (routine and manual occupations) infant mortality is 5.9 infant deaths per 1000 live births. This is 20 per cent higher than the average 4.9 per 1000. Disadvantage early on in life can lead to lower educational achievement, which can itself mean lower wages and a lower pension. In this way, poverty can persist throughout a lifetime. The Scottish Index of Multiple Deprivation (SIMD) found that more than two-thirds of the most deprived areas in Scotland are concentrated in Glasgow City, Inverclyde, North Lanarkshire, Renfrewshire, South Lanarkshire and West Dunbartonshire.

of a child's development – social, educational and personal chances – to a large extent.

One of the long-term problems with poverty is debt. Households with children are more likely than others to have levels of expenditure above their weekly income levels. The cumulative effect of this is social exclusion which can be passed on from generation to generation. Just paying for school uniforms, activities, trips and so on can cost, on average, about £1000 a year for a secondary school pupil. Both parents and pupils report that they suffer from considerable disadvantage in school due to these extra costs. School holidays are an additional challenge with the cost of entertaining the children and the loss of free school meals.

Poverty also shapes the development of a child. Before reaching their second birthday, a child from a poorer family is already more likely to show a lower level of attainment than a child from a better-off family. Children growing up in poverty are more likely to leave school at 16 with fewer qualifications.

Children who get five GCSEs at A*–C grade

Children eligible for free school meals
35.5%

Children not eligible for free school meals
62.9%

The Joseph Rowntree Foundation calculates that a family of two parents and two teenage children needs £430 a week after housing costs to have a reasonable standard of living. The Government poverty line for such a family is £352. But a family with the father working full time on minimum wage, and after receiving every benefit due to them, has to survive on just £308.

Figure 3.3 A teenager experiencing social exclusion ↑

Fact File

Child poverty in the UK: Key facts and figures

- In 2008–09, 2.8 million children were living in poverty. This is about 30 per cent of children.

- 2.2 million children (17%) were in both low income and material deprivation in 2008–09.

- 40 per cent of poor children live in a household headed by a lone parent. However, the majority (57%) live in a household headed by a couple.

- 38 per cent of children in poverty are in families with more than three children.

- 1.9 million children live in workless households.

- In 1999, Tony Blair committed to ending child poverty by 2020. This equates to a government target of 1.7 million to be lifted out of poverty by 2010. However, only 600,000 children were lifted out of poverty between 1998 and 2008.

- Child poverty costs the Exchequer £25 billion each year.

- Eradicating child poverty requires action in a wide range of policy areas such as child care, skills, availability and flexibility of jobs, benefits and tax credits.

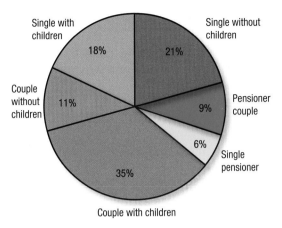

Figure 3.4 Make-up of the poor population by household status, 2008–09 ↑

What are the causes of child poverty?

Worklessness is the key factor leading to child poverty. Worklessness among lone parents is very common, with about two in five not in work. This results in rates of poverty for children in lone-parent families being high. Three-quarters of lone-parent families who found work escaped poverty after two years. There is also a high proportion of workless lone mothers who live in social rented housing. Families that experience high rates of income poverty include those with poor paternal health, material deprivation,

worklessness, low education, no private transport and that are living in overcrowded accommodation.

Worklessness is the result of three main changes. Firstly, the number of lone-parent families has increased, most are headed by women and most of these women are not in paid work. Secondly, unemployment levels are rising. Thirdly, male inactivity rates have risen substantially especially for men aged 25–49.

Finding work or increasing the number of hours worked is not a straightforward option for all families, especially those with very young children. Child care services and finding sustainable jobs are important considerations for parents with young children.

'**Worklessness is a cancer which eats away at children's future prospects as they grow up believing – as they do – that the world of work is nothing to do with them: that work and careers are only for people like you and me.**'

Martin Narey, RSA Speech, 19 January 2011

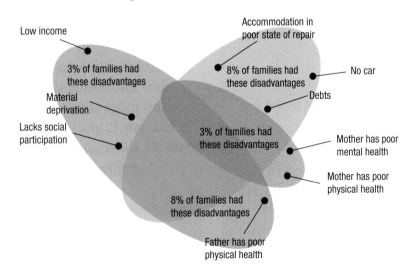

Figure 3.5 Cluster analysis identified families with similar combinations of disadvantages ↑

Source: National Centre for Social Research: Child Poverty in Britain: Causes and Consequences, August 2010

'Working poor' households

Around 60 per cent of 'working poor' families have children and more than 80 per cent of these are couple families (rather than lone parents). Half of working couples where neither partner is working full time are living in poverty, as are a fifth of lone parents working part time.

There are, however, more children in 'working poor' households. More than 60 per cent of poor children now live with parents who work, showing that poverty is not simply a result of worklessness. Almost all of the impoverished working families have two parents and many are families where the father has a job and the mother stays at home to bring up the children. A key feature of the recession has been the lower than predicted rise in joblessness. Workers have opted for pay freezes, reduced hours and voluntary redundancies rather than compulsory lay-offs. But the other side has been lower earnings for many people in work and this has contributed to higher levels of in-work poverty. The Government's welfare reform plans stress that work is the best route out of poverty but without action to tackle low pay, improve job quality and help parents progress in work it is difficult to make progress on tackling child poverty. Chapter 4 will look at strategies and ideas to deal with the issue of child poverty, and their effectiveness.

Nick Pearce, Director of Institute for Public Policy Research (IPPR), said in September 2010:

'While unemployment increased by less than expected in the recession, these figures clearly show that being in work is no guarantee of being out of poverty.'

Activities

1 Examine Figure 3.4. Which groups are at most risk of income poverty and why might this be the case?

2 What evidence is there for the extent of child poverty?

3 What are the causes of child poverty in the UK today?

4 What evidence is there to show that poverty is not necessarily a result of 'worklessness'?

5 'The Government's welfare reform plans stress that work is the best route out of poverty.' Why might this statement be flawed? Use evidence to support your answer.

Older people

Figure 3.6 An elderly person experiencing fuel poverty ↑

Until the last few years, the proportion of pensioners living in low income households had fallen sharply from 29 per cent of all pensioners in 1998–99 to 14 per cent in 2008–09. The fall has been sharp for single pensioners as only 18 per cent are now in low income households compared with 37 per cent ten years ago. The proportion of pensioner couples in low income households has also fallen, from 22 per cent to 15 per cent.

Pensioners over the age of 75 are more likely to live in low income households than younger pensioners. Very few low income pensioners have a very low income (below 40% of median household income). This is all based on low income threshold that deducts housing costs. Many older people own their homes outright and so they have low housing costs. Counting the number of people in receipt of guaranteed Pension Credit is the best indicator available for the geographic distribution of low income among pensioners. More than twice as many people are in receipt of this in Glasgow than in most of the rest of Scotland.

In Scotland, around 140,000 pensioners have no income other than the State Pension and other state benefits. This amounts to about one in four single pensioners and one in thirteen pensioner couples. The proportion of workers without a current pension (either in a pension scheme run by their employers or a pension they have arranged themselves) increases as household income decreases. Two-thirds of those in the poorest fifth do not have a current pension. Most workers aged 24 or under do not have a pension.

In the UK about a third of all pensioner households entitled to Pension Credit are not claiming it (1.3 million households). Two-fifths of all pensioner households entitled to Council Tax Benefit are not claiming it (1.7 million households). This has risen substantially over the last decade (26% to 33% for Pension Credit and 29% to 40% for Council Tax Benefit).

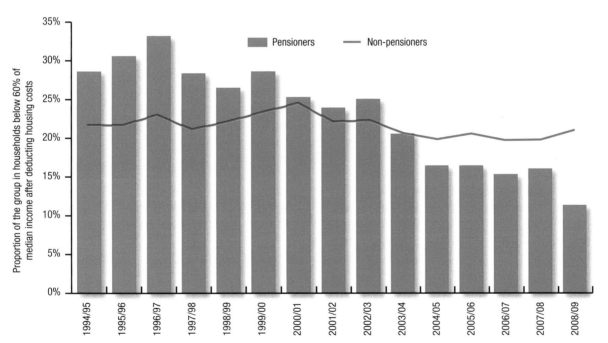

Figure 3.7 With substantial falls over the last decade, pensioners are now much less likely to be living in low income than non-pensioners ↑

Source: Households Below Average Income, DWP, September 2010

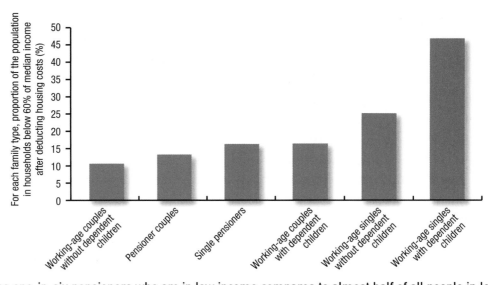

Figure 3.8 The one-in-six pensioners who are in low income compares to almost half of all people in lone-parent families ↑

Source: Households Below Average Income, data average for 2006–07 to 2008–09, DWP, September 2010

Causes of poverty for pensioners

It is difficult to identify the main causes of poverty in relation to older people. Research indicates that older people who had undertaken further education had greater material resources (see box below for explanation) than those who hadn't. Men have higher levels of material resources than women. Older people who were married had higher levels of material resources compared to those who were not. Older pensioners had fewer material resources than younger ones. Good health correlated with higher levels of material resources.

Material resources

There are many ways of defining this. For the purpose of this section the definition is as follows.

Material resources include: employment status, variety of sources of income, home ownership, paying for one's own food and whether the person had private health care insurance.

It has been found that poverty in old age is determined by earlier life experiences, especially having a job and the subsequent ability to save and invest. Once older people move into material deprivation there is very little they can do about their position in later life. This can lead to social exclusion. Older people with low levels of material resources or income are over-represented by women, persons living alone, those who are widowed, divorced or separated, in poor health, with a lower education and living in deprived neighbourhoods.

Fuel poverty and pensioners

One of the problems facing many pensioners is fuel poverty. The term 'fuel poverty' has become increasingly well publicised in recent years as energy prices rise. This has left many households being unable to afford to heat their homes to a comfortable level. It is pensioners who have felt the brunt of this. This is partly due to their typically lower incomes than other, younger households but also due to the fact that older people are more likely to spend more time at home. Older people also require a slightly warmer room temperature in their homes.

The official definition of fuel poverty is when a household must pay more than 10 per cent of its disposable income to heat their home to an adequate level. For older people this is defined as 23°C in the living room and 18°C in other rooms. Fuel poverty is determined by three key factors: income poverty, home energy efficiency and energy prices. In the past few years, energy prices have increased and this has led to dramatic increases in fuel poverty.

In the UK, fuel poverty for single pensioner households stands at about 58 per cent. Recent research in Scotland has shown that in March 2009 about a third of people aged 55 and over had turned down their heating during that winter because they were concerned about the cost. In social groups D and E (the groups most likely to experience poverty) the percentage rose to 43 per cent. The Scottish Government is legally obliged to eradicate fuel poverty as far as is possible by 2016.

The effects of fuel poverty on pensioners

Fuel poverty can damage the quality of people's lives and health. The likelihood of ill health increases in cold homes with illnesses such as flu, heart disease and strokes all exacerbated by the cold. The need to spend a large part of income on fuel means that fuel-poor households may have difficulty buying other household essentials and this can lead to poor diet and/or withdrawal from the community. About half of the excess winter deaths are circulatory in cause, due to low temperatures. In the UK from December to March, there are between 20,000 and 50,000 excess deaths compared to the rest of the year.

Poverty and unemployed young adults

The unemployment rate for 16–24-year-olds is now more than three times the rate for older workers. In the mid-1990s, it was twice the rate for older workers. As a result, two-fifths of all those who are unemployed are now under 25. Averaging across 2008–10, the unemployment rate was higher for young men than for young women: 20 per cent compared to 15 per cent. This contrasts with those aged 25 to retirement where the rate is similar for men and women. The unemployment rate for 16–24-year-olds in 2010 in Scotland was higher than its previous peak in 1993. Unemployment of young people, especially in cities, can lead to a host of major societal issues – poverty, social exclusion, physical and mental wellbeing of the individual through to drug abuse and related crime. Jobseeker's Allowance claimants peaked at 1.6 million in 2009. The Government has many challenges in this area: in-work poverty, the number of young adults with few/no qualifications, young adult unemployment, health inequalities and low income households' lack of access to essential services.

A great deal of research has gone into investigating the issue of this so-called 'lost generation'. The research has been about those who 'fail' and why they do so; the so-called 'disaffected', 'detached', 'disconnected'; the 'NEETS', 'the hard to reach'. It looks at social exclusion through the eyes of the young people growing up in some of the poorest areas in Britain. These young people suffer from 'multiple

Figure 3.9 The 'lost generation' ↑

deprivation' – joblessness, benefit dependency, ill health, crime, problematic drug use, poor skills/qualifications. It is not hard to make the links between the situation of these young unemployed adults and poverty/social exclusion.

The low-pay, no-pay cycle

'Just jumping from job to job, it's no way to go. It's a nightmare! Jack of all trades, master of none [laughs]. I just want something with a bit of job security – where maybes I can buy me own house in the future rather than just where you've got to be on a wing and a prayer type thing ... just a job that I can call me own, you know what I mean? Rather than just looking for one all the time or just jumping from job to job.'

(Richard, 30)

Source: 'The low-pay, no-pay cycle: understanding recurrent poverty', Prof. Tracy Shildrick and Prof. Robert MacDonald, Social Futures Institute, Teesside University, 9 March 2011

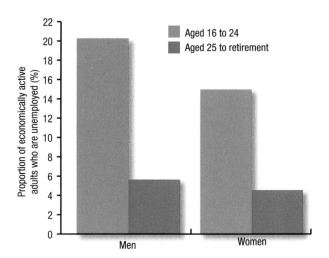

Figure 3.11 The unemployment rate is higher for young men than for young women ↑

Source: Labour Force Survey, ONS UK, March 2011; the data is the average for 2008–10

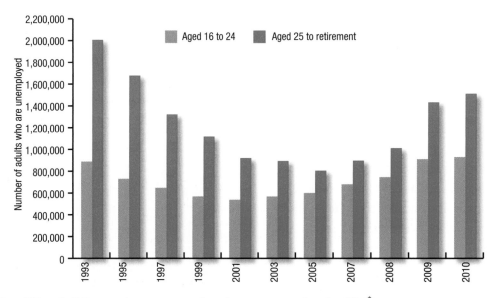

Figure 3.10 Two-fifths of all those who are unemployed are now aged under 25 ↑

Source: Labour Force Survey, ONS UK, March 2011

Activities

1   What evidence is there that older people suffer more from poverty than some other groups in society and to what extent has this situation changed in recent years?

2   What are the main causes of pensioner poverty?

3   Why is fuel poverty an issue for some older people?

4   What are the effects of fuel poverty on pensioners?

5   Why do most unemployed young adults face poverty?

6   What evidence is there to show the extent of their poverty?

Regions and poverty

Poverty levels vary across the UK. Generally, poverty appears to be greater in the North compared with the South. This is reflected in the lack of available jobs in areas of deprivation. Three of the ten hardest places to find employment in Britain are in Scotland, with West Dunbartonshire topping the list of employment blackspots (see Table 3.2). This places a significant question mark over the Government's welfare reform strategy to enable the long-term unemployed to return to employment – 'What jobs?' might well be the question asked in towns like Dumbarton.

Fact File

The challenges of poverty

- In one in four families in Scotland nobody works. In the UK as a whole, the figure is one in five.

- Scotland's youth unemployment rate has risen faster than for the UK as a whole.

- In Scotland, 200,000 young people who left school between 2003 and 2007 have never held regular work since.

- Life expectancy in Scotland is among the lowest in Europe, with men expected to live until 76 and women until 80.

- Health researchers put the average male life expectancy in Easterhouse at 66.

- Save the Children says 90,000 Scots youngsters live in households that survive on less than half the median income, with nearly 75 per cent of the children being part of families in which no adult works.

- The problem is most pronounced in Glasgow, where 18 per cent of youngsters live in severe child poverty. This is double the Scottish average.

- Glasgow is the lowest performing local authority in education, with only 16 per cent of students gaining three Highers compared with 34 per cent Scotland-wide.

- 30 per cent of Glasgow children qualify for free school meals compared with the Scottish average of 14 per cent.

Source: Adapted from the *Sunday Times*, May 2011

Figure 3.12 Dumbarton and its famous Rock   ↑

The figures in Table 3.2 illustrate the challenge facing Iain Duncan Smith and his 2011 Government White Paper on Welfare Reform (see Chapter 4).

Table 3.2 **Number of unemployment benefit claimants per job advertised in local job centres**

Area	Number of claimants
West Dunbartonshire	40.3
East Ayrshire	32.8
Haringey	29.3
North Ayrshire	28.2
Lewisham	25.9
Hackney	25.9
Greenwich	22.9
Eilean Siar	21.3
Isle of Wight	19.1
Lambeth	19.1

Source: Office for National Statistics, May 2011

In August 2010 the Scottish Government produced a report called *Relative Poverty across Scottish Local Authorities*. The publication, for the first time, presents the official figures about the distribution of income and relative poverty across all Scottish local authorities. These figures have been produced using the Scottish Household Survey (SHS).

The statistics produced by the report are complicated but they do show that Dundee City has the lowest net equivalised household income before housing costs (equivalisation means they have taken into account the size of the family so they can make more meaningful comparisons). The highest household income can be found in Aberdeenshire (there is a difference of almost £7000). In Dundee, the percentage of households in relative poverty is 24 per cent, while in Aberdeenshire it is 16 per cent. Glasgow City is about 22 per cent. The Scottish average is 19 per cent.

The charity Save the Children revealed in February 2011 that 12 per cent of the young people in Dundee were growing up in deprived living conditions – the national average is 9 per cent. Glasgow City was top with 18 per cent. At present, there are thirteen people chasing every job in Dundee – this is higher than in Glasgow City where there are eleven.

Shettleston man

The media reports at the time of the Glasgow East by-election in 2008 and the General Election in 2010 showed poverty as an individual responsibility. This encouraged the stereotyping of benefit recipients such as 'Shettleston man'.

Iain Duncan Smith on Shettleston man: 'This individual has low life expectancy. He lives in social housing, drug and alcohol abuse play an important part in his life and he is always out of work. His white blood cell count is killing him directly as a result of his lifestyle and its lack of purpose.' Smith also alludes to the fact that Shettleston man's lifestyle is down to his individual failure and personal responsibility. He also suggests that 'the welfare system has become part of this breakdown, giving perverse

Figure 3.13 **Kilmarnock in East Ayrshire** ↑

incentives to too many people. It needs to be changed. It needs to have a simple purpose: to move people from dependence to independence … At the heart of this lies work. The system must help people to not only find work but also to remain in work, to get the work habit.'

The reality TV programme *The Scheme* allowed viewers to pass judgement on the lives of people in a disadvantaged community in Kilmarnock. However, it did not take into account the devastating economic change in the Kilmarnock area nor contexts of widening social inequalities. The focus of the programme was on one housing scheme and on particular individuals within it, in isolation from the wider issues surrounding poverty and inequality across Scotland and the UK. The programme focused on the generation of specific cultural lifestyles that keep people in poverty.

Activities

1 What evidence is there of wealth inequalities in different parts of Scotland?

2 Why are some areas more prosperous than others? Use some case studies to support your answer.

3 Using the example of 'Shettleston man' as described above to help you, devise your own descriptions of different groups that face poverty. Your descriptions must be based on relevant and current evidence. This should act as a summary for you.

Essay questions

1 To what extent is poverty an issue in the UK?

2 To what extent is there a North–South poverty divide in Britain?

Measures to Deal with Inequalities in Wealth

Poverty is about not having enough resources. Income is the main resource lacking.

The central theme of the Labour Government's social policy from 1997 to 2010 was to promote social inclusion in order to re-engage those people who were in poverty and had become detached from work, education, health and community. The Labour Government designed its social policy around programmes and strategies that would get the unemployed off welfare and into work. From 1997, successive Labour Governments tried to do this through a number of strategies.

To increase levels of employment:

- Working Tax Credit (WTC)
- Child Tax Credit
- National Minimum Wage (NMW)
- New Deal
- Modern Apprenticeships.

To help the income levels of those not in work:

- Jobseeker's Allowance (JSA)
- Jobcentre Plus
- Pension Credit
- Winter Fuel Payment.

Strategies to increase levels of employment

Tax credits

The Labour Government of 1997 had a long-term goal to halve child poverty by 2010 and abolish it within a generation. Tax credits were central to this strategy. Tax credits are payments from the Government. The Budget of 2000 confirmed that the Labour Government would be reforming the way families with children and those in work on low incomes would be supported through the tax and benefit system. The reforms created two new tax credits: Child Tax Credit, which is a single system of support for families with children that is paid directly to the main carer in a family; and Working Tax Credit (WTC), which is paid through the pay packet to working people without children as well as families with children. These credits were designed to tackle child poverty and help to ensure that work paid more than welfare and that people had incentives to move up the earnings ladder. The WTC aimed to tackle persistent poverty among working people.

There was also a debate about the most appropriate way to support families with children through the benefit system. There were those who argued that support should be provided universally and others who favoured a targeted means test. The tax credit was a way to support all families with children while offering the greatest help to those who needed it most through what was called a 'light touch' income test. The old means-testing approach compelled families to run down any savings before they could get help from the state. A tightly targeted means test only helped the very poorest, leaving many low-to-middle income families without appropriate financial support. These tax credits have been judged to be better than what they replaced for the following reasons:

- more money
- less form filling
- simpler administration and more responsive system
- fairer system: less scope for people to 'play the system'
- better incentives for dual-earner couples
- better incentives to save
- support for children is paid to the main carer.

According to the independent think tank, the Institute for Fiscal Studies, the Labour Government's main taxation and welfare benefit changes since 1997 have managed to halt rising inequalities but failed to significantly reverse the growing gap in incomes between rich and poor that opened up during the Thatcher and Conservative years of 1979–97. Income inequality in Britain rose by 40 per cent between 1979 and 2001, a larger increase than in any other developed country. The gap between rich and poor was greater in 2002–03 than it was in 1996–97 when Labour came to power.

> 'Since 1998, New Labour's large, real terms increases in means-tested welfare benefits and tax credits have significantly reduced inequality, but have not so far been sufficient to offset the effect of two decades during which benefit rates lagged behind earnings growth.'
>
> Source: Institute for Fiscal Studies

What strategies might be most effective in reducing poverty?

- Invest more in skills training and life-long learning for all households especially those of low income families.
- Make the tax system more progressive, i.e. raise the higher rate of tax from 40 per cent for the top earning households.

- Look carefully at the effects of changes in indirect taxes such as VAT in case they have a regressive effect on the overall distribution of income.
- Focus more on targeting benefits by means testing them.
- Increase the value of welfare benefits/tax credits in line with the annual percentage growth in median earnings.

The agreement among researchers is that high employment and a commitment to raise the skills and potential earnings of people towards the bottom of the pay ladder are the most effective and sustainable policies in the long term.

National Minimum Wage (NMW)

In October 2011 the National Minimum Wage (NMW) increased as follows:

- over 20s: up 15p (2.5%) to £6.08
- 18–20: up 6p (1.2%) to £4.98
- 16–17: up 4p (1.1%) to £3.68
- apprentices: up 10p (4%) to £2.60.

Figure 4.1 Vince Cable, Business Secretary ↑

Comments about this rise

Business Secretary Vince Cable said that the changes would help more than 890,000 of Britain's lowest-paid workers.

The UNITE union commented that the increase would do little to help low-paid workers keep up with rising food and fuel prices.

The British Chamber of Commerce said that the changes risked pricing young people out of work when youth unemployment was at a record high. The Chamber's David Frost said, 'These changes will be a barrier to job creation and ultimately economic recovery.'

Why was the National Minimum Wage introduced?

The long-term aim of a minimum wage was to remove the problem of poverty pay that exists when earnings from paid work do not result in a living wage and fail to push people out of poverty. It was introduced because of:

- increasing income inequality
- increasing child poverty
- increasing burden on the Exchequer of in-work benefits.

The National Minimum Wage was introduced in April 1999. Since then it is estimated that about 1 million people a year benefit from the annual rise in the NMW.

Figure 4.2 Less-skilled workers benefit from a national minimum wage ↑

What has been the impact of the NMW?

Members of the Political Studies Association recently voted the NMW the single most successful government policy of the last 30 years. The Coalition Government has declared its support for it. But the recession and its subsequent recovery have not affected all groups of workers equally. Many of the groups of workers most likely to have minimum wage jobs have fared quite well in the last two or three years. Women have fared better than men, ethnic groups better than white people, older people better than those aged between 35 and 54, and disabled people better than those without disabilities. Young people and those without qualifications have fared particularly badly in the recession.

The impact of the NMW varies considerably across sectors. One in ten women benefits from a NMW compared to 4 per cent of men. One in five under-25s have had their wages boosted by NMW.

However, a third of those benefiting from NMW are not heads of households but young people living at home or married women living with employed husbands.

The Low Pay Commission Report (independent of the Government) has claimed that the NMW has helped to reduce the gender inequality gap, arguing that women more than men have been lifted into a higher wage rate since 1999. The report also claims that due to the prevalence of women in part-time jobs as well as low-paying jobs, the NMW plays a more important role and has a greater impact on raising women's earnings in comparison to those of men. The report also claims that the gap between ethnic minority workers and white workers has been significantly reduced. See Figure 4.3.

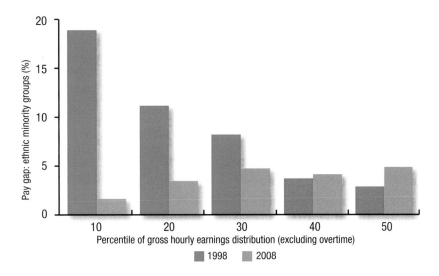

Figure 4.3 Pay gap between white and minority ethnic workers in the UK, 1998 and 2008 ↑

Source: House of Lords Library Note: Debate: National Minimum Wage and Poverty, 11 March 2010

Arguments in support of and against the NMW

Arguments against the NMW

- It raises the cost of employing people so firms will cut jobs, reduce hours of work for employees and unemployment will rise.

- Other workers may want higher wages as well and this will increase the total wage bill and damage the price competitiveness of UK companies in the world market.

- Young and low-skilled workers still lose out as companies tend to employ older workers who have more experience.

- A NMW will not necessarily ease poverty because many poor households do not have a low-income earner. Poverty tends to be concentrated in groups where no one is in paid employment. It would be better to introduce a minimum income guarantee.

Arguments to support the NMW

- Greater equality will be achieved and the pay gap will be narrowed.

- Poverty may be reduced as the low paid get more money and the unemployed may be encouraged to get jobs because the higher wage is an incentive for individuals to work.

- Less exploitation by employers who pay below the minimum wage.

View of the Scottish Low Pay Unit

'Poverty in the workless population is well documented and being tackled by the Government in its welfare to work policies. Yet poverty among low-paid workers remains a pressing issue. For those who need it most – including those providing essential services such as childminding, cleaning and catering – the National Minimum Wage has made little real difference, nor is the tax credits system making real inroads.'

As argued by Carol Murray from the Scottish Low Pay Unit

The Scottish Low Pay Unit believes that an adequate level of NMW would assist the Government's anti-poverty strategy but that it would also fail to tackle the root cause of in-work poverty (where workers do not earn enough to survive). They recommend that research be carried out to establish a 'living wage' level on which to base the NMW. They think that, in the meantime, a universal flat-rate NMW based on at least half of male median earnings would be a help to eradicate poverty.

Activities

1 What are tax credits and why did the Government of the time think that tax credits were central to their child poverty goals?

2 How successful have these strategies been? You may need to research this further.

3 To what extent has the National Minimum Wage (NMW) helped to alleviate poverty in the UK?

4 What are the arguments for and against keeping the NMW and for introducing a living wage?

Case Study: Living Wage Campaign

In May 2011 the London Citizens, made up of church groups and trade unionists, held a rally celebrating ten years of its London Living Wage Campaign. The campaigners were appalled at the living conditions of many of London's low-paid workers. Ken Livingstone, former Labour mayor of London, referred to the campaigners as 'the best example of the Big Society'. Even David Cameron during the 2010 election campaign described the living wage as 'an idea whose time has come' though he has yet to follow through a pledge to introduce it for ancilliary staff across Whitehall. London Citizens has persuaded many major employers to agree to pay their London staff well above the minimum wage – the target for 2010–11 was £7.80. The campaign has now gone UK-wide. The Scottish Poverty Alliance (SPA), trade unionist and church groups have been calling on firms to introduce a living wage in Scotland (the target set was £7.00). Glasgow City Council introduced a living wage of £7.00 an hour in 2009 to its lowest paid employees and Scottish Enterprise now ensures that all their directly employed staff are paid at least £7 an hour.

Figure 4.4 The Living Wage Campaign ↑

New Deal

Lone parents and their children are one of the most vulnerable groups in the UK. The number of lone parents and the incidences of poverty and unemployment among them were high in 1997. In addition, child poverty and teenage pregnancy had become more common and are often

Fact File

Welfare policies

Over the years, there have been a number of welfare policies affecting lone parents. Some of these are:

1997   Child maintenance bonus payments on movement into full-time work. Ended 2009.

1998   New Deal for Lone Parents

1999   Family Credit replaced with Working Families' Tax Credit to supplement income of working parents.

       Increase in basic level of income support.

       Introduction of National Minimum Wage.

2001   Target set to get 70 per cent of lone parents into work by 2010.

       Introduction of Jobcentre Plus.

2003   New Child Tax Credit and Working Tax Credit begin.

2004   Income Support ends for lone parents whose youngest child is aged 12 or over.

2009   Income Support ends for lone parents whose youngest child is aged 10 or over.

       Introduction of Flexible New Deal. This involved a more personal approach to ensure that customers got the extra support to find work.

2010   Income Support ends for lone parents whose youngest child is aged 7 or over.

associated with lone parenthood. There is also agreement that these issues are closely linked to parents' employment.

In response to these issues, the New Labour Government introduced the New Deal for Lone Parents (NDLP) as part of its package to address inequality in the UK. New Deal is a programme aimed at providing lone parents with the required support to move from Income Support into the labour market, in line with the USA 'make work pay' approach to welfare. It was the first UK labour policy specifically targeted at lone parents. New Deal also has programmes for other groups including New Deal for Young People (NDYP), New Deal 25+ and New Deal 50+. Since NDLP and other measures came into place, lone parents have increasingly moved into employment and relative poverty among lone parents has substantially declined. There is also the belief that parents' employment will have positive effects for their children in terms of health gains, and improved behavioural and educational outcomes.

The impact of NDLP and other interventions targeting lone parents

Government evaluations tend to focus on short-term impacts such as the number of lone parents who move into jobs and in/out of Income Support. But the main purpose of programmes such as NDLP was to raise family income and living standards in the long term. However, a 2003 evaluation (Lessof *et al.*, 2003) found that NDLP had a large positive impact on entries into work. After six months, 43 per cent of participants had got a job compared to 19 per cent of non-participants.

There is limited evidence of the impact of lone-parent programmes (LPPs) on children. A 2009 study *Work and Wellbeing over Time* said that children associated mother's work with financial reward. They saw employment for their mothers as an opportunity to meet friends and get out of the house. Child care was often said to be inappropriate and unsuitable. A British Lone Parents Cohort report suggested that, compared to children from working households, 11–15-year-olds from non-working households were more likely to frequently truant from school, to have been in trouble with the police and to have a negative attitude to doing well in school. In conclusion, this evidence has been based on the fact that lone parents and their children registered disproportionately high poverty rates and that this could be reduced by integrating lone parents into the job market. The evaluations concluded that the NDLP and other measures have been effective in helping lone parents to find a job and so there are fewer claiming benefits. However, it seems to be that Working Tax Credits (in general terms) with top up earnings have had more of an impact than NDLP.

Activities

1 Lone parents can be a very vulnerable group with regard to wealth inequalities. Why did the previous Labour Government set up the New Deal for Lone Parents (NDLP)?

2 In what ways might NDLP help families get out of poverty?

3 To what extent has NDLP been successful? Justify your response.

4 What other groups of people may be helped by the New Deal programme?

Modern apprenticeships

In the April 2011 budget George Osborne, the Coalition Government's Chancellor of the Exchequer, promised an extra 40,000 apprenticeships for young unemployed people in response to rising youth unemployment. He said that more employers should run on-the-job training schemes (in the UK only one in ten businesses does so, while in Germany, Austria and Switzerland one in four employers offers the scheme). The budget also announced that an additional 80,000 work experience placements would be created by 2013 (on top of the 20,000 already announced). These would give young people direct experience of work. Official figures showed that one in five 18–24-year-olds was out of work.

There has been a lot of comment since the Coalition Government made this announcement. Some employers think the apprenticeship drive is 'unrealistic'. Normally the word 'apprentice' means a young male in overalls and safety goggles working in trades such as plumbing or building. We don't tend to think of apprenticeships in service sector jobs such as retail or accountancy. The Federation of Small Businesses (FSB) said that companies would be unable to provide all the extra places that the Government wants because each apprentice had to get up to 280 hours of teaching away from the workplace and that other requirements were just as onerous. Peter Winebloom from EEF (the manufacturers' organisation) said that, 'the Government's aims are laudable but there is an issue with employers being able to offer apprenticeships when they are still twitchy about the [economic] outlook and the margins are

Figure 4.5 A young apprentice ↑

Case Study: Batchelor Polyurethanes

Joanne Batchelor, director of small manufacturing firm Batchelor Polyurethanes based in Birmingham, said she has been put off hiring apprentices due to the 'horrendous' cost involved.

She had wanted to recruit a 19-year-old onto a four-year engineering apprenticeship starting in September 2011, but said there was 'no funding or help whatsoever' when she enquired. The cost of training alone would have reached £150,000, she said.

When asked what stopped her going through with the placement, she said, 'The cost and the fact he would have had to go away to do some classroom-based training.'

tight. Employers don't want to take apprentices on only to lay them off.' Business groups such as EEF were disappointed that the Government had not introduced financial incentives such as tax credits for taking on apprentices.

It is therefore difficult, at this stage, to assess the effectiveness of this scheme in dealing with inequalities in wealth in the UK.

Government schemes to help the income levels of those not in work

Below is a list of government schemes to help those not in work:

- Jobseeker's Allowance (JSA)
- Jobcentre Plus
- Pension Credit
- Winter Fuel Payments.

Jobseeker's Allowance (JSA)

An evaluation of the impact of JSA on wealth inequality in the UK

There is not much researched evidence on the impact of JSA in recent years. Much of the research focused on comparing the previous unemployment benefit with its replacement, the JSA.

Fact File

What is Jobseeker's Allowance?

JSA is part of the UK's social security benefits system. It is meant to cover the cost of living expenses when the claimant is out of work.

To get it, you must be:

- available and actively seeking work
- aged 18 or over but under State Pension age
- working less than 16 hours a week.

It is paid at the end of every fortnight straight into the bank/building society.

The amount a person would get varies but on average (April 2011) the amount is:

Aged 16–24   £53.45

Aged 25 +   £67.50

To claim JSA, a person must attend an interview at the Jobcentre. Here a 'jobseeker's agreement' will be drawn up that will set out what steps need to be taken to find work. Attendance at fortnightly (or thereabouts) reviews is essential.

Presently, the number of women claiming unemployment benefit is at its highest since records began in 1997. The number of people (aged 18+) claiming JSA in January 2011 was 1,459,700, an increase of 2400 since December 2010. The number of males claiming has fallen for twelve consecutive months but it has increased for females for the previous seven months.

Anna Bird of the Fawcett Society, which campaigns for gender equality in the UK, stated she was worried about the disproportionate effect of these figures on women. She said that to cut back the public sector workforce would hit women hardest since 65 per cent of workers in that sector were women and they were concentrated in the low paid, low grade and insecure jobs.

There is an argument that the amount of the JSA needs to be substantially increased. It amounts to half of the Pension Credit and two-thirds of the State Pension. Based on this, it can be concluded that the JSA is low. Relative to the average level of consumption, JSA is now worth half of what it was worth 30 years ago.

The social security argument is that a civilised society needs a system that provides an acceptable level of financial support for people who cannot support themselves. In 2009 Ipsos MORI, a market research company, undertook a survey on behalf of the Department of Work and Pensions (DWP) that showed firm support. The report said that, 'All participants strongly supported the provision of state support and financial benefits for those in need.'

The low level of JSA has led to 70 per cent of all adults in workless unemployed families being in poverty. This is considerably higher than the percentage of lone parents and those who are sick or disabled. One reason to increase JSA, therefore, would be that a substantial majority of those who would get it would otherwise be in poverty.

Jobcentre Plus

As stated on the DWP website, Jobcentre Plus is a government agency supporting people of working age from welfare to work and helping employers to fill their vacancies.

Fact File

Jobcentre Plus Annual Report 2009–10

'The demand for our services remained high with around 600,000 more new claims for Jobseeker's Allowance in 2009–10 compared to the previous year. Every working day we continued to help well over 5000 people into work.

For customers as they became unemployed:

We continued to help the newly unemployed get up to date with the latest job search techniques through:

- access on day one to individually tailored job search assistance for customers needing specific help immediately, in overcoming barriers to finding and keeping work

- a new one-hour group information session on job search techniques

- a new one-day advice and coaching session delivered by external providers, including some specific advice for those looking for professional or executive jobs.

We provide further support to the newly unemployed in getting them back to work through a series of additional temporary measures:

- access to specialist help in CV writing, interview preparation, debt and money advice, confidence building and work skills

- support

- help with their rent

- help with their mortgage interest payments, depending on income, for those who were unemployed for over thirteen weeks.'

Source: http://www.dwp.gov.uk/docs/jcp-annual-report-and-accounts-2009-2010.pdf

Figure 4.6 A Jobcentre Plus branch ↑

Pension Credit

This is money for some people aged 60 and over. It has two parts: guaranteed credit and savings credit. Guaranteed credit tops up your weekly income to a guaranteed level. It is means tested and depends on how much income and savings you have. For example, a person can get the guaranteed credit if their weekly income is below £137.35 a week. You would also get other benefits such as free health care, Cold Weather Payment, maximum Housing Benefit and Council Tax Benefit.

According to figures published by Turn2us in April 2011, the majority of older people are not aware that they may be able to claim Pension Credit. The research showed that about half of pensioners asked were struggling to make ends meet. Nine out of ten of them knew that Pension Credits existed but only two out of ten claimed it.

Winter Fuel Payment

When a person reaches pension age they receive the universal benefit of a Winter Fuel Payment. For winter 2011–12, the amount for a person under 80 is £200. This is a reduction from the previous year. In England, it is estimated that 25,000 more households will be in fuel poverty as a result of this reduction. The main universal benefit that the elderly receive is the State Pension.

The Scottish context

In the aftermath of the decline of traditional industries such as coal mining, steel and shipbuilding, the Scottish economy turned into a largely service sector economy. This led to a change in types of jobs for the workforce. Its most devastating impact has been on uneducated, young workless men.

Prior to the 2008 recession, record numbers of people in Scotland were in employment but many still faced income poverty. It is the opinion of some academics that it is not the lack of employment or a lack of wealth that has caused poverty in Scotland but that the policies have failed to reward paid employment appropriately and have failed to distribute resources fairly among the population. A living wage is required and benefits and tax credits should be increased to help people avoid poverty. Some academics believe that progress towards combating poverty has been undermined by the Coalition Government's approach to reducing public expenditure (see page 39).

The 2010 *Growing Up in Scotland* report found that a quarter of three-to-four-year-olds and a fifth of five-to-six-year-olds were living in 'persistently poor' families. Recent policies have had a positive impact on poverty in such families by making it easier for parents of young children to continue to work. The introduction of tax credits and increased benefits have raised the incomes of these groups. The Treasury's Sure Start programme increases to maternity and paternity leave and the entitlement to universal, free, part-time nursery education for three-year-olds in 2004 all helped to deal with child poverty. In Scotland there was also a limited scheme offering free nursery places for disadvantaged two-year-olds. However, the Coalition Government, in its emergency budget in autumn 2010, pledged to ensure that child poverty would not increase – but not to reduce it. Child Benefit was frozen for three years.

The SNP Government in Scotland set out a joint framework with local authorities for tackling poverty, called 'Achieving our Potential'. This included, for example, tackling pay inequalities in the public sector and extending free school meals to children in working families with the lowest incomes. But there are grave concerns about how these national initiatives are translated into action at local level. More recently, ministers have committed to ensure that all directly employed Scottish government staff and NHS workers receive a 'living wage' (see page 32).

2011 and the future?

Unprecedented spending cuts, due to the recession, mean that the future for all people

Activities

1   How useful are Pension Credit and Winter Fuel Payments in helping older people make ends meet? You need relevant evidence to support your answer.

2   What are the main causes of poverty in Scotland in recent years?

3   Assess the effectiveness of Scottish Government strategies in dealing with issues such as poverty. Justify your answer. You may need to research this further.

4   Copy and complete the following table with as much detail as possible. This should help you sort out the information you have.

Group of people suffering from poverty	Causes of poverty	Evidence of poverty	Strategies to deal with the problems	Effectiveness of the strategies	Evidence to support effectiveness
Children					
Older people					
Lone parents					
Unemployed					

who live in poverty looks bleak. But this should not be a barrier to further progress. Spending needs to focus on ensuring that low income families have a fairer share and that services are delivered in a way that does not exclude children. While Westminster controls crucial employment and social security factors (reserved powers), Scottish and local governments need to do their best to improve the quality of employment opportunities, the distribution of pay and the approaches to other services such as child care. The creation of a more equal Scotland will have benefits for all people living in Scotland.

The Welfare Revolution

In October 2010 Chancellor George Osborne announced that in the lifetime of this Parliament £81 billion of cuts would be made to reduce the massive budget deficit, which he blamed on Labour rather than the banking crisis of 2008 and world recession. He also announced that the welfare budget would be cut by £18 billion by 2015 and this was designed to incentivise people back to work (see Fact File on page 40).

Figure 4.7 Chancellor George Osborne states: 'It will always pay to work. Those who get work will be better off than those who don't.' ↑

However, given the extent of public sector cuts and redundancies for public sector workers, it is difficult to accept that there are sufficient jobs for the unemployed to find. Chancellor Osborne stated that the private sector will provide the new jobs required, which might well be the case for the prosperous areas of the South of England but is unlikely to be so for Scotland and the North of England. He also stated that £2 billion of the welfare cuts would be used to simplify the welfare system (see 'Reform of the welfare system' on pages 40–41).

Critics of the Chancellor argue that he is concentrating on the workshy who often appear in newspaper articles highlighting how much they receive in benefits (see 'Families are draining the taxpayer over generations' on the next page). The Institute for Fiscal Studies (IFS) argues that the Government's fiscal and welfare policies, such as the increase in value added tax (VAT) to 20 per cent, will hit the poorest households more than those in the upper-to-middle of income distribution. Again state and public sector pensions are now linked to the Consumer Price Index instead of the Retail Price Index and this is not beneficial to people's pensions. The ending of the universal Child Benefit (see Table 4.1 on page 41) could be the Government's first step in removing all universal benefits, such as the State Pension.

Helen Dent, Chief Executive for the organisation Family Action, suggests that 'cuts to welfare support and services mean that life is tough and the future is looking bleak. Warm words on social mobility, child poverty, early intervention and parenting support will not be enough to save children from a life in poverty.' She also suggests that cuts to housing support, freezing Child Benefit, increasing VAT from 17.5 per cent to 20 per cent, the end of Educational Maintenance Allowance (EMA) in England and cutting back on the Social Fund are all hitting families hard. In conclusion she states, 'the Coalition is failing families – they need to work harder'. In support of Helen Dent, Imran Hussain, who works with Child Poverty Action Group, also says that the Government is failing children. Child poverty will not end by 2020 and much of this is due to £18 billion of benefit cuts including a three-year freeze on Child Benefit and housing and disability benefit cuts. The IFS predicts that both relative and absolute child poverty will have risen.

The Government would argue that measures to increase the personal allowance threshold will benefit the low paid as they will pay no tax or witness a reduction, resulting in 850,000 of the lowest paid being taken out of income tax. Again they would argue that the middle class are being hit harder with, for example, the non-payment of Child Benefit to 40 per cent tax payers (see Table 4.1).

Reform of the welfare system

Iain Duncan Smith, the Secretary for Work and Pensions, wishes to simplify and integrate benefits to create one universal credit. The first stage of the planned reform would be to bring all benefits together under one 'universal' credit using a new 'real-time PAYE tax system'.

Secondly, those who went back to work would have their present benefits withdrawn more

Case Study: Families are draining the taxpayer over generations

In 2010, the Government spent £192 billion on social welfare. More than 3400 families were receiving Housing Benefit of £26,000 a year alone. Families where three generations live on benefits are becoming increasingly common.

In 2008, the McFadden family from Ellesmere Port, near Chester, had a brief moment of infamy when it emerged that three generations of adults in their household were not working. Neither Sue McFadden, a 58-year-old divorcee, nor two of her three daughters, all single mothers bringing up six children between them, nor McFadden's oldest grandson, Kyle, were in work. The family was living on benefits of more than £32,000 a year with no prospect of supporting itself.

Fact File

Budget cuts

- Total welfare spending in Britain has increased from £132 billion in 2000 to £192 billion in 2011.
- The proportion of people living on benefits has increased from 5 per cent in the 1960s to 29 per cent in 2010.
- The annual amount spent on Jobseeker's Allowance, Housing Benefit and Income Support (the three most common welfare payments) is £30 billion.
- The annual bill for the Disability Living Allowance is £11.5 billion – more than the entire Home Office budget.
- There are 5.9 million people on out-of-work benefits, with 1.4 million receiving these payments for nine out of the past ten years.

Adapted from *Sunday Times*, 25 July 2010

slowly, to ensure that people would always be better off working.

Thirdly, benefit would be linked to a desire to work. Choosing not to work if you are capable would not be accepted.

Creation of jobs is central to ensure that the long-term unemployed enter the job market. However, as Ian Bell stated in the *Herald* (13 November 2010), 'Neither Mr Duncan Smith nor anyone else has explained how these legendary multi-generational tribes of welfare-dependent scroungers are fit for work, even if the work existed.'

Figure 4.8 Iain Duncan Smith states: 'We are trying to redo the welfare system to get it back to what Beveridge originally wanted. He wanted to reward work, for work to be the route out of poverty. We have 5.5 million people of working age who are simply not working. This is a terrible indictment.' →

Table 4.1 What is happening to middle-class benefits?

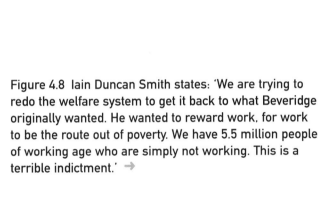

	Child Benefit	**Child Tax Credits**	**Health in Pregnancy**	**Child Trust Fund**
What is it worth?	£2449 for three children	£545 'family element'	£190 per child	£250 top-up age 7
How many claim it?	7.7 million	5.8 million	750,000	4.4 million
How much does it cost?	£12 billion	£5.6 billion	£150 million	£500 million
What changed?	Higher-rate taxpayers will no longer receive it from 2013	From April 2011 households earning more than £40,000 no longer receive it	Scrapped from 1 January 2011	Scheme closed to new children from 1 January 2011

Case Study: No country for the disabled and ill?

David Cameron is determined to reduce the number of claimants on Employment and Support Allowance (ESA), formerly called Incapacity Benefit (IB). Those on IB receive higher payments. The Government wants to reassess all current Incapacity Benefit claimants by 2014, including the 81,670 people claiming the allowance as a result of health problems stemming from alcohol, drug and obesity conditions. Individualists would argue that these are life choice issues and that these people are incapacitated through their own fault.

David Cameron stated, 'There are many in our country who can't work because they are incapacitated through no fault of their own. There are many others who, with help, can work. But there are some who are on these benefits who do not deserve them.'

The opposition parties argue that with the Government reducing public expenditure a massive number of public sector workers are losing their jobs. As such there will be no jobs for those IB individuals now assessed as fit to work.

The £100,000 million a year contract to reassess people claiming disability and sickness benefit was awarded to the French-owned Atos Healthcare. In a pilot study that included Aberdeen, almost 30 per cent of claimants were informed they were fit to work. The private company's doctors have since begun the UK process. The *Sunday Mail* revealed in March 2011 that Atos told an undercover GP they treated people like 'claimants, not patients'.

The Glasgow headquarters of Atos has been referred to as 'Lourdes' by many of those who have been reassessed – they go in sick and come out 'cured' and are placed on lower-paid Jobseeker's Allowance.

- A 63-year-old man was assessed as fit for work two months after having a heart attack.
- A 50-year-old man who has lung disease was told he could work after being examined for less than ten minutes.

Child Benefit to be axed for higher-rate taxpayers from 2013

At the October 2010 Conservative Party Conference, Chancellor George Osborne announced that from 2013 couples where one parent earns about £44,000 would no longer receive Child Benefit. It is estimated that this will affect about 1.2 million families and save £1 billion a year. At present an estimated 7.7 million families with children currently get Child Benefit, costing about £12 billion a year.

During the 2010 general election campaign the Conservatives had promised to retain Child Benefit as a universal benefit because, according to George Osborne, it was 'valued by millions'. However, at the 2010 Conference he stated: 'Believe me, I understand that most higher-rate taxpayers are not the super-rich. It is very difficult to justify taxing people on low incomes to pay for the Child Benefit of those earning so much more than them.'

At present, families receive £20.30 a week for the eldest child and £13.40 for subsequent children, with payments continuing until the age of 19 for those in full-time education.

Critics of this decision argue it is unfair – the cut will especially hit homes with one single high earner and a partner staying at home to care for the children. Families with three children who will no longer be eligible for Child Benefit could potentially become £2500 a year worse off.

In contrast, families with two parents each earning up to £44,000, which could add up to a total of over £80,000, would still keep the benefit. In defence of this the Chancellor said that his plan was 'the most straightforward' option and would avoid the need to introduce a 'complex' system of means testing, whereby all UK households would have their incomes assessed.

Labour claimed this marked the end of the principle of universal benefits that have underpinned the Welfare State for decades. Shadow Work and Pensions Secretary Yvette Cooper stated, 'We support Child Benefit for all children and all families. Whatever people's income, it is families with children who are paying most – through cuts in Child Tax Credit, Maternity Allowance, Child Benefit and Housing Benefit.' The Child Poverty Action Group also criticised the decision, saying that it was 'unfair' that families should be made to pay the price for a debt crisis that was not of their making.

Activities

1   Why is the Coalition Government reforming the welfare system?

2   What impact will welfare cuts have on all sections of society?

3   What changes are taking place to ESA and Child Benefit and why are these controversial?

4   What is the difference between universal and means-tested benefits? Give examples.

Essay question

Critically examine the success of recent government policies to reduce poverty.

5 Causes of Health Inequalities

One of the fundamental principles on which the NHS was based in 1948 was a commitment to remove inequalities in the provision of health care. Yet, despite the achievements of the NHS, there is clear evidence that a person's social position, ethnic origin, gender and the area in which they stay can affect their chances of achieving good health.

There are many influences on an individual's health, for example biological factors, personal lifestyle, the physical and social environment, and health services (see Figure 5.1). For this reason, care must be taken before concluding that geographical or social class, or other factors, are the key to explaining differences in mortality (death) rates or morbidity (illness) among individuals or groups.

Figure 5.1 Factors influencing health ↑

From 'Inequalities in health in Scotland: what are they and what can we do about them?' by Sally Macintyre, Medical Research Council: Social and Public Health Sciences Unit, October 2007

Geographic inequalities

In February 2006 a Health Inequalities Study by Caci, an information service company, made the headlines in all Scottish newspapers. The system used by Caci measures alcohol consumption, smoking, exercise, weight and long-term illness. It draws on official information, as well as private sector market research, and can identify individual streets with a particularly high concentration of unhealthy residents. The headline in *The Herald* summed up its depressing statistics: 'Scotland: sick man of the UK with 22 of the top 25 illness areas'. A previous national survey by Bristol University in 1999 had provided similar banner headlines when *The Daily Record* highlighted the North–South divide: 'Shock report reveals the poorest places in Britain are all in Scotland'. While both surveys emphasised the geographical divide, the reports clearly identified poverty as being the main culprit.

There is a clear North–South divide in the health of the British public. According to numerous government statistics 'death rates are highest in Scotland followed by the north and north-west regions of England'. A 2009 report by the Commons Public Accounts Committee highlights the wide disparities in cancer care and death rates across the UK. Scotland has the highest death rate from lung cancer – almost twice the death rate in the south-west of England. Also life expectancy for men and women is lower in Scotland compared to

England and Wales (see Tables 5.1 and 5.2). The life expectancy gender gap across the UK has narrowed. Over the past 27 years the gap has narrowed from 6.0 to 4.2 years.

These differences cannot be explained through a disparity in health care expenditure and health service employees. In fact, Figure 5.2 clearly shows that spending on health in Scotland is significantly higher than in England – annually more than £200 extra per person is spent on health care in Scotland – yet people who live in Scotland experience more ill health. Staffing levels in health care are also about 30 per cent higher than those in England. Scotland suffers greater social deprivation and has a lower percentage covered by private health care. Again for geographic reasons, it costs more to supply the same level and quality of service in Scotland than in England. Scotland has less than 10 per cent of the UK population but about 33 per cent of its land area. In addition, Scotland has numerous island communities that need to be provided with adequate health care services.

Table 5.1 **Life expectancy, 2009**

	Male	**Female**
Scotland	75.4	80.1
England	78.0	82.1
Wales	77.1	81.4

Table 5.2 **Age-standardised deaths per 100,000 population**

Region	**Men**	**Women**	**All**
East	185	119	152
East Midlands	217	139	178
London	215	129	172
North East	242	151	196
North West	258	158	208
Northern Ireland	241	151	196
Scotland	287	174	230
South East	189	119	154
South West	197	119	158
Wales	238	145	191
West Midlands	230	140	185
Yorkshire and The Humber	224	147	186

Source: UK Government Health Statistics, 2010

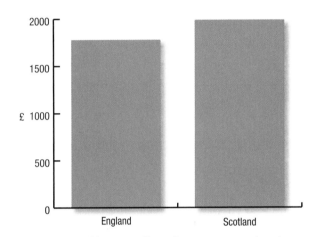

Figure 5.2 Health expenditure by country per head, 2009–10 ↑

Caci Report 2006

The Caci Report confirmed the shockingly unhealthy lifestyles of a significant number of Scots. The report found that Scots are more likely to suffer long-term illness, take less exercise, be more overweight and spend more on cigarettes and alcohol than other Britons.

By concentrating on precise wards within urban and rural areas, the report was able to highlight pockets of health deprivation within wealthy areas. Aberdeen, regarded as a prosperous city, had five wards in the UK's top 25 unhealthy areas. As was expected, Glasgow had six areas in the 'league table' and Dundee three, thus underlining the link between urban deprivation and ill health. Phil Hanlon, Professor of Public Health at Glasgow University, stated, 'This study confirms our efforts are having an effect in some areas, but not in the poorest areas.'

The Bowbridge area in Dundee had the dubious honour of being the most unhealthy area in Britain. All of Britain's 25 healthiest wards are located in the Home Counties of England with most concentrated in the London commuter belt. Newcastle West (worst area number 13) is England's most unhealthy ward in which spending on tobacco averages £415 a year per person and 47 per cent of residents are overweight.

The survey once again highlights the North–South health divide. Significantly, all of the worst areas are in run-down housing estates either on the periphery of a city or in the inner city.

Figure 5.3 Bowbridge is one of the 22 areas in Scotland that rank among Britain's unhealthiest ↑

Local differences

Recent research in this area, however, has indicated that basing policies on the principle of tackling inequalities is much too simplistic an approach. There are areas in Scotland and

northern England, for instance, that compare favourably with the healthiest areas in the south-east of England, while parts of London have records of poor health comparable with the most deprived areas in the country.

It is clear that social class and lifestyle play a crucial role. This is highlighted in the findings of numerous government and health reports such as the WHO Report of 2008 (see pages 47–48).

Social class inequalities

The Black Report

Numerous reports have highlighted the link between poverty and poor health. The most famous was the Black Report in 1980 and unfortunately most recent reports confirm that its findings are still relevant today.

This enquiry into *Inequalities in Health* established for the first time a clear link between different socio-economic groups and health. Sir Douglas Black, President of the Royal College of Physicians, used the classifications defined by the Registrar General. The Black Report concluded that while the health of the nation had improved, inequalities in health between the higher and lower social classes was widening. Class inequalities in health could be traced from childhood and continued throughout life.

The report concluded that the Government should take a more active role in encouraging changes 'in people's diet, exercise and smoking and drinking behaviour. Greater emphasis should be given to preventing ill health rather than curing it and a first step should be a ban on smoking in public places' (see pages 52–53).

The 1998 Acheson Report

In 1997 the new Labour Government set up a Commission under the chairmanship of Sir Donald Acheson, the former Chief Medical

Officer for England and Wales, to investigate health inequalities in the United Kingdom.

The report provided a comprehensive survey of the condition of the disadvantaged and its conclusion echoed the Black Report – poverty had to be tackled through concerted government action and a policy of social inclusion in education, housing, employment, social services and health provision.

The report summarised the lives of 9 million adults and 2 million children in the following way:

'The poor were unhealthy. They did not live as long and they suffered more from lung cancer, coronary heart disease, strokes, suicide and violent accidents than their richer peers. These inequalities had steadily worsened over the preceding twenty years. They were more likely to have their cars stolen and their homes vandalised. They ate less iron, calcium, dietary fibre and vitamin C. They were fatter. Their homes were colder.'

There has been little significant improvement since the Acheson Report was published.

WHO Report 2008

In 2008 the World Health Organisation (WHO) provided further evidence of the link between deprivation and poor health. *The Herald* in its article on the report had as its headlines

Figure 5.5 Calton (top) and Lenzie (bottom) ↑

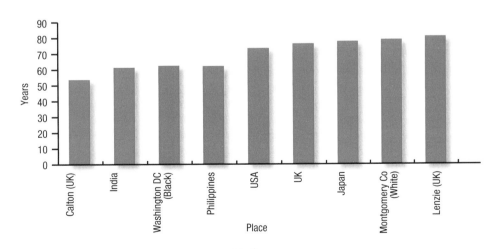

Figure 5.4 Male life expectancy at birth around the world ↑

Source: World Health Organisation, 2008

'Poverty takes 30 years off your life'. The WHO report had carried out a three-year analysis of the 'social determinants of health'. The report concludes 'social injustice is killing people on a grand scale'. For instance, a boy in the Calton district of Glasgow's East End is likely to live to 54 but just a few miles away in the prosperous suburb of Lenzie, average male life expectancy rises to 82. The report admits that there has been an improvement in people's health over the last decade but the benefits to the worst off have not been as significant as those seen among the best off.

Figure 5.4 clearly illustrates the contrast in life expectancy and the fact that the people of India have a higher life expectancy than the people of Calton.

Centre for Population Studies

Recent research from the Centre for Population Studies indicates that the cycle and extent of poverty has a biological effect, which means that generations of families who live in areas of deprivation are more likely to succumb to illness. This is one hypothesis that Glasgow Centre for Population Studies, which is running the study, is trying to test. Scientific links between physiological changes, such as tissue inflammation, and mental tension are being investigated. A separate report by a group of researchers on *Geographical Variation in Mortality by Social Class* provides some evidence to support the above hypothesis. What is interesting about this report is that it uses socio-economic status to compare mortality rates across the UK.

The most significant finding is the variation across the UK in health for social class V (the group most likely to suffer from poverty). The social class V figure for heart disease is almost

double in Scotland compared to that in England, while the Scottish figure is significantly greater for all cancers. A key question is why, coming from a similar poor socio-economic background, is the health of the Scots so much worse (see the Three Cities Report 2010 on page 51)?

Life expectancy gap is widening

Figures released by the Registrar General for Scotland in September 2010 further confirmed that the disparity in health between people in the richest and poorest areas had widened over the preceding decade (see Table 5.3).

The people who live longest in Scotland live in East Dunbartonshire, just a few miles from the boundaries of Glasgow which has the lowest life expectancy for men at 71.1. In contrast, the male figure for East Dunbartonshire is 75.8. Glasgow has the lowest female life expectancy rate of 77.5 years. The good news for Glasgow is that health has improved and life expectancy for men has increased by 2.6 years. The bad news is that the health gap with East Dunbartonshire has widened. In 1999 the gap for women was 4.0 years; in 2009 it had widened to 5.6 years.

On the positive side the statistics conclude that the people of Scotland, including those in Glasgow, are living longer and that the life expectancy gap between the sexes has narrowed. Overall life expectancy for the genders has increased to 75.4 and 80.1 for men and women respectively. The gap in life expectancy has been reduced from 5.5 years to 4.7 years.

A spokesman for the Scottish Executive welcomed the overall improvement in health while stating that 'the main problem is persistent health inequalities across Scotland, and improving everyone's health while tackling these inequalities is the main priority'.

Table 5.3 Figures for male and female life expectancy at birth in Scotland from selected local authorities

	Male		Female	
Scotland	**72.7**	**75.4**	**78.2**	**80.1**
Council Areas	*1997–99*	*2007–09*	*1997–99*	*2007–09*
Aberdeen City	73.7	75.7	79.3	80.6
Aberdeenshire	75.1	78.0	80.0	81.4
Dundee City	73.7	71.7	77.7	79.4
East Dunbartonshire	78.3	75.8	79.5	83.1
East Renfrewshire	76.3	77.8	80.7	82.0
Edinburgh, City of	73.6	76.9	78.9	81.5
Fife	73.8	76.1	79.1	80.4
Glasgow City	68.5	71.1	75.5	77.5
Highland	73.0	76.3	79.1	81.2
Inverclyde	69.7	73.1	77.7	79.0
North Ayrshire	72.5	74.0	77.8	79.2
North Lanarkshire	71.4	73.7	77.0	78.5
Orkney Islands	73.4	75.5	79.5	81.7
Perth & Kinross	74.8	78.2	79.5	81.8
Renfrewshire	71.0	73.7	77.5	79.2
Scottish Borders	74.9	77.1	79.6	81.2
South Lanarkshire	72.5	74.9	77.7	79.9
West Dunbartonshire	69.9	72.5	76.7	78.4

Source: Register General for Scotland, 2010

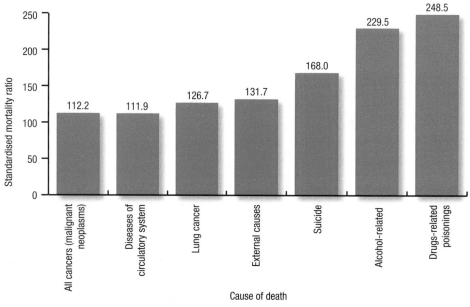

Figure 5.6 Glasgow (top left), Manchester (top right) and Liverpool (bottom) have similar poverty-related issues ↑

Figure 5.7 Standardised mortality ratios 2003–07 for Glasgow relative to Manchester and Liverpool (combined) for seven causes/groups of causes ↑

Source: *Journal of Public Health*, 2010

Three Cities Report 2010

Further evidence of the complexity of the causes of health inequalities appeared in the *Journal of Public Health* in March 2010. The research examined the health and death rates of the citizens of Glasgow, Manchester and Liverpool between 2003 and 2007, cities with broadly similar deprivation figures. The headline in *The Herald* 'Blame Glasgow effect for city's chronic ill health – not deprivation' clearly indicated that lifestyle, not just poverty, was to blame.

Fact File

- In Glasgow about one-quarter of the population are classed as deprived. Manchester and Liverpool have similar profiles.
- There are 900 extra deaths per year in Glasgow compared to Manchester and Liverpool.
- Deaths among the most wealthy were 15 per cent higher in Glasgow than in the other two cities and 18 per cent higher among the most deprived.
- Figure 5.7 clearly indicates that Glasgow's cancer and heart disease deaths are well above those of Manchester and Liverpool.
- More disturbing are the alcohol- and drugs-related deaths in Glasgow – more than double the figures of the other two cities.

These findings confirm the research by Professor Phil Hanlon of the University of Glasgow Centre for Population Health. This points to a Glasgow/West of Scotland effect in which the combination of decades of unemployment with factors including family, poverty, chronic stress, relationship issues, attitude and behaviour, and damage to physical and mental health results in early deaths for adults in these areas.

The Herald concludes: 'We cannot casually blame it on our genetic inheritance or the climate and this research shows we can no longer put it down to poverty, so we must change our behaviour.'

Lifestyle issues

It is clear that poverty is a major factor in explaining health inequalities. However, this cannot explain why the health of Scots in areas of deprivation is worse than that of their counterparts in England. As indicated in the Three Cities Report, lifestyle is also an important factor. Unhealthy diets and obesity, cigarette smoking and drugs and alcohol – all lifestyle choices – play a crucial role in one's health.

The rise in the number of overweight children is a phenomenon common to the western world, and is based on a diet of high fat junk food and a dramatic reduction in physical activity. Furthermore, a recent international report reveals that Scottish boys are growing fatter than their counterparts in England and are heading towards becoming the fattest in Europe. One in eight Scottish children is classified as officially overweight.

Children with two obese parents run a 70 per cent risk of becoming obese, compared with a risk of less than 20 per cent among children with two lean parents. In 1996, 10 per cent of children in the UK were obese with the figure increasing to 18 per cent by 2010.

Social class and obesity

A careful examination of the socio-economic distribution of people in Britain who are overweight confirms that fat is also a class issue. The lowest social class has levels of obesity that match American levels, while the highest social class has the lowest obesity levels.

In 2008, only 33 per cent of women aged 16 and over took the recommended level of physical activity. Men were better at 45 per cent. Therefore two-thirds of women chose not to exercise adequately. Only 56 per cent of girls under 16 took sufficient exercise, which compares badly with other European countries. So the pattern appears to be continuing.

Lifestyle choices include levels of exercise, diet and eating junk food, alcohol consumption and smoking. Only one-quarter of women ate the recommended five portions of fruit and vegetables per day. Again this is affected by income. Only 13 per cent of women in the least deprived 20 per cent of the population ate five portions per day compared to 28 per cent of women in the top 20 per cent of the population.

It is estimated that obesity costs the NHS in Scotland £457 million every year. The drug bill alone is £5 million with about 12,000 Scots taking the obesity drugs. At present, an estimated 3400 people die in Scotland as a direct result of obesity every year. The scale of the problem is reflected in hospitals spending tens of thousands of pounds on specialist beds that can take patients weighing 39 stones and up.

Lifestyle and smoking

Smoking is a crucial factor in the ill health of people who live in deprived areas. Smoking is a class issue, as Table 5.4 indicates. In 1960 there were no significant differences in the smoking habits of all social classes in the UK. The award-winning TV series *Mad Men*, set in 1960s affluent America, depicts all the top executives as being smokers. However, by the 1990s the professional classes had listened to health advice and the number of smokers in social class I had fallen by 75 per cent. In contrast, the number of smokers in social class V had dropped by only 30 per cent.

A time bomb is ticking which, in the long run, will impact on the lifespan of females. Professor Stephen Spiro stated that Glasgow had one of the worst records for lung cancer among women. He said, 'More women die from lung cancer in

Table 5.4 Cigarette smoking status, among adults, by socio-economic classification, 2008

Current cigarette smokers	All classifications (%)	Managerial and professional (%)	Intermediate (%)	Routine and manual (%)
All adults	21	15	20	26
Men	22	16	21	28
Women	19	14	18	24

Source: General Household Survey, 2009. Office for National Statistics

Table 5.5 Cigarette smoking by gender, 2008

	Men (%)	Women (%)
England	22	19
Wales	21	20
Scotland	24	24

Source: General Household Survey, 2009. Office for National Statistics

Glasgow and Liverpool than anywhere else in the UK. Women are twenty years behind men in their smoking habits. Men were struck down with vicious (lung) cancer years ago and now the pattern is moving on. It is women who will now be experiencing this vicious type of lung cancer. For women booking into antenatal clinics, 36 per cent of those from the most deprived 20 per cent of the population were smokers compared to 6 per cent who were in the least deprived 20 per cent.

It is clear that smoking is one factor that explains the different mortality rates between the social classes.

Table 5.4 clearly indicates that smoking is an issue linked to social class and poverty. In 2008, 48 per cent of adults in deprived areas of Scotland were smokers, a higher proportion than in deprived areas of England and Wales where the figure was 41 per cent. As stated, this geographic difference can be explained by poverty and lifestyle. This explains why the Scottish Government banned smoking in public places in 2006 (see page 62). Every year there are more than 13,000 smoking-related deaths in Scotland alone.

Figure 5.8 An unhealthy lifestyle ↑

Alcohol and drug abuse

Excessive consumption of alcohol leads to ill health with increased likelihood of illnesses such as cirrhosis of the liver and high blood pressure. Parts of Scotland are blighted by a booze culture which, according to the NHS, kills 40 Scots a week.

Total recorded alcohol consumption doubled in the UK between 1964 and 2009. The 2010 Scottish Health Survey echoed a 2010 NHS Scotland report which indicated that Scots are more likely than drinkers elsewhere in Britain both to binge on alcohol and exceed the recommended daily intake. Daily alcohol consumption in Scotland for both men and women is 25 per cent higher than in England. Average weekly consumption for men is 43 units, which is more than double the official recommended intake.

A further major concern is the increase in the number of young people who drink to excess. Ian Gilmore of the Royal College of Physicians stated that it had once been unusual to see serious alcohol-related liver damage before the age of 40. Now people in their thirties or even twenties are showing signs of such damage. The youngest person found to have alcohol-related liver damage was a seventeen-year-old who started drinking at the age of twelve.

The SNP Minority Government failed in November 2010 to have its proposals to tackle alcohol abuse approved by the Scottish Parliament (see pages 65–66).

Scotland also faces a serious drugs problem. According to a 2009 United Nations report Scotland is ranked second out of 47 European countries for heroin, cannabis and ecstasy use. The same report shows that 3.8 per cent of people in Scotland consume cocaine, compared with 2.3 per cent in England and Wales.

Activities

1 To what extent is there a North–South divide in the health of the UK public and is finance to blame?

2 Outline the evidence that supports the view that social class/poverty is a crucial factor in health inequalities.

3 What conclusions does the Three Cities Report make?

4 What problems do obesity, alcohol and cigarettes create for an individual's health?

5 What evidence supports the view that lifestyle is a social class /poverty issue?

Gender inequalities

The gender gap in health was summarised by Miles in 1991 and is still relevant:

'Women live longer but suffer from more health problems in their lifetime.'

The causes of death, moreover, vary between men and women for different age groups. In the 1–14 age group, for instance, nearly twice as many boys as girls die from accidents and violence, while in middle age, deaths from lung cancer, heart disease, accidents and suicide are the major reasons for males' higher mortality rates.

In Scotland, the major cause of death in women is lung cancer rather than breast cancer. While breast cancer is still more common, the recovery rate is far higher than for lung cancer. The smoking habits of females over the last 25 years are causing concern and there is fear that the number of females who die from lung cancer will increase. Evidence from the statistics division of NHS Scotland in October 2010 supports this concern. In 2008, 2348 females were diagnosed with lung cancer compared to 1521 in 1985. In contrast the corresponding figure for men shows a decrease from 3294

in 1985 to 2462 in 2008. In October 2010 *The Herald* newspaper report on the above figures had as its headline: 'Health toll of ladette culture is laid bare – cancer figures reflect impact of drinking and smoking in 1980s.'

Mortality

Life expectancy is a commonly used indicator of health and women live longer than men across all social classes. The life expectancy of women in the most deprived social class is lower than for males in the least deprived.

Differences in life expectancy reflect biological and social differences. Men are more likely than women to die prematurely from heart disease and have higher death rates from lung cancer, injuries, poisoning and suicide.

In the UK, the most common causes of death in both men and women are cancer and circulatory diseases. However, women are more likely than males to die from strokes when they are much older and males get heart attacks at an earlier age. Women have higher death rates for conditions that are related to increasing age.

Men tend to be employed in more dangerous occupations than women so are more likely to die early from diseases or injuries connected with their work. Pressures on men from social expectations and norms mean that they are more likely to suffer from health problems and death related to smoking, alcohol and fast driving.

Male deaths as a result of road accidents are nearly three times the number for women and more men die from lung cancer due to higher rates of smoking, as well as cancer of the stomach and colon. The number of male deaths from chronic liver disease and cirrhosis was nearly twice the number of female deaths.

Women's traditional domestic responsibilities lead them to suffer from higher levels of anxiety and depression compared to males, particularly if they are poor and are lone parents. Women are two to three times more likely than men to be affected by depression or anxiety. Although men are more likely than women to die of injuries, women are more likely to die of injuries sustained at home.

Women are more likely to report illness at an earlier stage and are therefore more likely to make use of their doctor and be admitted to hospital. Women and men also differ in their patterns of health-related behaviour. For example, men have traditionally smoked more cigarettes and consumed more alcohol than women.

Morbidity rates

While women live longer, they also suffer from more ill health than men. Figures in the General Household Survey suggest that women in the lowest social class group report more than twice the rate of illness as women in the highest group.

Employment status seems to be another factor affecting women's health. With regard to women with children, middle-class women who have paid employment suffer less illness than women from the same class who stay at home, while working-class women with a paid job have worse health than those who do not. Finally, women appear to suffer disproportionately from mental illness, although fewer single women have psychiatric problems than married women. For males the reverse is true – mental health tends to be best among married men.

Towards an explanation?

Why do women suffer more health problems than men? Although surveys have suggested that women are more likely to admit to and report illness, three other factors have been highlighted as being more significant explanations.

Biological

Women's role in human reproduction can cause ill health. Pregnancy, childbirth, menstruation, contraception, abortion and the menopause all play a part in the greater morbidity rate experienced by women. This is perhaps borne out by the fact that in the younger age groups more males than females report long-standing illness and this trend is only reversed in the fifteen-plus age groups. The increase in the rates of lung cancer among women, at a time when they are beginning to show decline among men, suggests that gender differences in morbidity may widen while differences in mortality may narrow.

Poverty

The link between poverty and ill health is well documented, and there is evidence to suggest that women are more likely to suffer from the effects of poverty than men. The reasons for this can be found in the position of women in our society. For example, women may have to accept low-paid jobs, head lone-parent families, and may be expected to take on the caring role for elderly and disabled relatives.

Income plays an important part in determining health. Women (24%) are nearly twice as likely to live in poverty in Scotland than men (13%). The life expectancy for women in the poorest constituency in Scotland is 75.9 years compared to 82.0 years for the average woman living in the most affluent parts of Scotland. Table 5.6, taken from figures published by the ONS in 2009, shows that across a range of diseases mortality rates increase for women lower down in the socio-economic groups.

Therefore social class and income have a significant impact on the health of women.

Table 5.6 **Mortality rates per 100,000 women in England and Wales, 2009**

NS-SeC group	All cancers	Lung and throat cancer	Breast cancer	Heart disease	Cerebrovascular, i.e. strokes, etc.	Respiratory disease	Digestive disease
1	75	7	26	5	5	4	6
2	77	9	25	7	7	6	9
3	73	9	22	9	8	7	12
4	87	14	23	11	10	9	12
5	102	17	27	18	12	15	18

Source: ONS, 2009

Ageing

In the UK, 70 per cent of those aged over 75 are women. Since the elderly experience more ill health than those in the younger age groups, it is hardly surprising that proportionately women should have higher rates of morbidity than men.

Women have more ill health. Women are expected to live around 70 years in good health and 10 in poor health, whereas men average 68 years in good health and 7 years in poor health.

Figure 5.9 An Asian mother and child ⬆

Ethnicity and health

Poverty

Just as in the general population, poverty has an important impact on health in ethnic groups. Those groups that have incomes closest to the white population average, such as Indians, Africans, Asians and Chinese, record health levels close to those of the white population. Those groups that are poorest record significantly poorer levels of health. For example, Pakistanis and Bangladeshis record health levels that are 50 per cent worse than whites, and Caribbeans are 30 per cent worse.

Reported ill health

Asians report greater levels of ill health than other groups in the population. Chinese are less likely than the general population to report poor health. However, it is only in the over-50 age group that there is any significant difference in long-term limiting illness between minorities and the majority population.

Diseases and diet

Ethnic minorities differ in their risk of suffering from certain diseases. Diabetes is a particular problem for Pakistanis and Bangladeshis, who are more than five times more likely to suffer from it than the white population. Indians of both genders are three times more at risk.

Pakistani and Bangladeshi men and women face a higher risk of heart disease than average whereas Chinese face a lower than average risk. Black Caribbean women also face a higher risk.

Diet has a significant part to play in these variations. Members of different ethnic groups may have different diets because of cultural differences or to meet religious requirements. The proportion of Chinese and Black African and Caribbean populations who report eating at least five portions of fruit and vegetables per day is higher than in the general population, whereas the proportion among the Pakistani community is lower.

Culture – smoking and alcohol consumption

Culture has a significant impact on lifestyle choice. For example, the Muslim religion does not permit the consumption of alcohol. Social customs among some groups do not approve of women smoking.

The 1999 Health Survey for England found that members of all minority ethnic groups were less likely to drink alcohol than the general population, and those who did consumed smaller amounts. Only 7 per cent of men in the general population were non-drinkers, whereas 13 per cent of Black Caribbean men, 30 per cent of Chinese men, 33 per cent of Indian men, 91 per cent of Pakistani men and 96 per cent of Bangladeshi men did not consume alcohol.

For women the figures were even higher. For example, 99 per cent of Bangladeshi women did not consume alcohol.

Overall, ethnic minorities suffer from fewer diseases linked to alcohol overconsumption such as cirrhosis of the liver.

Bangladeshi men are more likely to smoke than any other group, followed by Black Caribbean men. However, Indian, Pakistani and in particular Chinese men are less likely to smoke compared to the general population. The 2001 Health Survey for England found that: '27 per cent of men in the general population reported being smokers compared with 44 per cent of Bangladeshi men and 35 per cent of Black Caribbean men. Indian (23%), Pakistani (26%) and Chinese (17%) men were less likely to report being smokers.'

'27 per cent of women in the general population reported being smokers compared to 25 per cent of Black Caribbean women, 9 per cent of Chinese women, 6 per cent of Indian women, 5 per cent of Pakistani women and 1 per cent of Bangladeshi women.' Obviously smoking has a significant impact on health, particularly in the rates for cancer and respiratory problems.

All ethnic groups are less likely to engage in physical activity than the general population in both Scotland and England, which again will have an impact on injuries, weight and its attendant health problems.

Another example of culture having an impact on health is the impact of the Muslim festival of Ramadan on devotees who suffer from diabetes. Many Muslims fast for up to 30 days during Ramadan and this can mean problems for diabetes management as they must abstain from eating, drinking, taking oral medication and smoking from before dawn to after sunset each day. Taking medicine that is derived from a porcine (pig) source is an issue for members of both the Jewish and Muslim communities.

Barriers to accessing health care

Many members of the minority ethnic community fail to access health care because of poor English language skills. Often without interpreters, minorities have difficulty knowing what is available or explaining what the problem is so do not seek medical care. There are also cultural barriers. Different groups in the minority ethnic community have different ways of dealing with ill health and these might not be understood by health care professionals in the UK. For example, research has shown that the diagnosis of chronic illness may not be discussed in the South Asian community so they may find it difficult to accept care from someone outside their community.

Activities

1 Women generally live longer than men. How does this disadvantage them?

2 What evidence is there that poverty increases the risk of ill health for women?

3 Assess the impact of lifestyle choices on women's health.

4 Examine the differences in both mortality and morbidity for both males and females.

5 Higher levels of ill health among British minority ethnic groups can be linked to a number of factors. Provide evidence for each of the following:

   ● Poverty

   ● Lifestyle

   ● Access to health care.

Essay questions

1 Poverty is the main cause of health inequalities. Discuss.

2 To what extent is lifestyle choice the most important factor in explaining health inequalities?

6 Government Responses to Health Inequalities

The UK Labour Governments of 1997–2010 and the Scottish Governments of 1999–2011 identified poverty and its links with lifestyle as being a major cause of health inequalities. Health is a devolved issue and the Scottish Labour/ Liberal Democrat Coalition Governments (1999–2007) and the SNP Government (2007–) have done much to improve the health of the Scottish public. Labour and the Liberal Democrats can point to their *Working Together for a Healthier Scotland* strategy, which is reflected in the banning of smoking in public places in 2006, and the SNP to its *Equally Well* strategy, which is reflected in the introduction of free prescriptions in 2011, as key initiatives in tackling health inequalities. The UK Labour Government, through its welfare reforms as described in Chapter 4, has done much to reduce child poverty. However, the banking crisis of 2008 and the recent economic recession followed by the massive Conservative/Liberal Democrat Coalition Government cuts in public spending 2010–15 will make it difficult to maintain progress in the reduction of health and wealth inequalities.

This chapter will consider measures taken by the Scottish Government to improve the health of the Scottish people and to reduce health inequalities. While health is a devolved issue, the UK Government, in its economic measures, impacts on health spending in Scotland. In the period 2003–08, NHS spending in the UK significantly increased to bring UK health spending as a percentage of GDP in line with European levels. In England health spending rose from £34 billion in 1998 to £90 billion in 2009 and in Scotland from £4.6 billion to £10.3 billion in the same time period.

The Coalition Government has promised not to reduce health spending as part of its reduction in public spending. However, a modest increase in health spending is actually a significant cut as the NHS has a much higher rate of inflation than the economy as a whole. It offers a 24-hour service and the demands placed on it continue to increase – in short the NHS is a victim of its own success.

Tackling Scotland's health problems

In 1999 Scotland's restored parliament placed the issue of health inequalities high on its political agenda. It was guided by the 1998 Green Paper on Public Health, *Working Together for a Healthier Scotland,* and the 1999 National Review of Resource Allocation for the NHS in Scotland.

Working together for a healthier Scotland

Donald Dewar, the First Minister in 1999, declared, 'Our attack on ill health is a central part of our battle against social exclusion. Ill health and social exclusion are bound up together – ill health can stop you getting a job, for example, and being excluded can damage your health further.'

The Green Paper set out an action plan of cooperation between health authorities and local government that would tackle health, housing, education and environmental problems. The lottery provided £300 million to set up Healthy Living centres in deprived areas in an attempt to reduce heart disease, cancer, and smoking among the disadvantaged (see page 61).

The Conservative Party in Scotland continued to deny the link between poverty and sickness. Mary Scanlon, health spokesperson for the Scottish Conservatives, said, 'I think it's wrong to say that poor health is directly linked to poverty and low incomes. It is linked with poor eating and lifestyle habits which can be changed with greater public awareness.'

Setting health targets

The following health targets were set:

Top priority: to reduce premature mortality from coronary heart disease by half and from cancer by 20 per cent, saving the equivalent of more than 2500 lives in Scotland each year.

Smoking

Target: to cut smoking among 12- to 15-year-olds from 14 per cent to 11 per cent by 2010. Attempts to reduce the proportion of women smoking during pregnancy from 29 per cent to 20 per cent. Nicotine substitutes to be provided as free prescriptions and a new law to be considered on banning tobacco advertising.

Drinking

This is on the increase but there will be renewed effort to reduce the incidence of men and women exceeding weekly alcohol limits from 33 per cent to 29 per cent, and 13 per cent to 11 per cent, respectively. Reducing the percentage of young people drinking from 20 per cent to 16 per cent will form part of a more general drive to improve children's health.

Fair shares for all

The Arbuthnott formula, based on the 1999 National Review of Resource Allocation for the NHS in Scotland, plays a key role in tackling health inequalities. In 1999 the independent group reviewing Scottish health services, headed by Professor Arbuthnott, introduced 'a new funding allocation which benefits Scotland's poorest areas and rural communities'.

However, not all health boards are happy with the formula. NHS Grampian declared that the funding formula was 'morally and ethically unacceptable because boards such as Glasgow and Clyde are being financially rewarded for unhealthy lifestyles'. NHS Grampian receives the lowest per capita allocation of all the health authorities. Grampian has 10.3 per cent of the Scottish population, but receives only 9.0 per cent of NHS funding. While Grampian is regarded as an area of prosperity, Aberdeen suffers from inner city deprivation, which impacts on health.

In 2009–10 the Scottish Resource allocation formula was introduced to replace Arbuthnott and to allocate 70 per cent of the NHS budget to the fourteen NHS boards in Scotland. Deprivation is still a key factor in the allocation of resources.

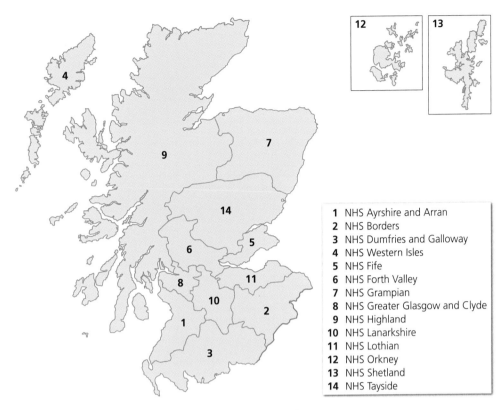

1	NHS Ayrshire and Arran
2	NHS Borders
3	NHS Dumfries and Galloway
4	NHS Western Isles
5	NHS Fife
6	NHS Forth Valley
7	NHS Grampian
8	NHS Greater Glasgow and Clyde
9	NHS Highland
10	NHS Lanarkshire
11	NHS Lothian
12	NHS Orkney
13	NHS Shetland
14	NHS Tayside

Figure 6.1 Map of Scotland showing the fourteen health boards ⬆

Case Study: Local initiatives to tackle health inequalities – Have a Heart Paisley

'Have a Heart Paisley' aimed to reduce heart disease and promote healthier, longer lives for the people of Paisley.

Applying lessons learned from previous activities, the project delivered a programme of work aimed at those most at risk of developing heart problems. With its partners in the community, the NHS and the local authority, Have a Heart Paisley aimed to demonstrate through these programmes the degree to which preventive measures can improve heart health by tackling risk factors and unmet treatment needs.

Emerging lessons from the work of Have a Heart Paisley helped to guide future policy and practice in the prevention and treatment of heart disease throughout Scotland. The Heart Health Learning Network plays a key role in the dissemination of these lessons throughout the country.

Have a Heart Paisley Project Manager Cath Krawczyk said, 'The project focuses on preventing the development of heart disease among the working age people of Paisley.'

What has been achieved?

This section will examine the impact of the above policies and strategies in tackling health inequalities. Vigorous and controversial measures have been taken against smoking and tackling obesity, especially in the young, and binge drinking is a high priority. The decision to restrict smoking has led some health specialists to advocate greater government intervention in controlling the drinking and even eating habits of the Scottish public (see pages 63–67).

Smoking ban

It was hoped that the smoking ban in enclosed public places (pubs, restaurants and other public places) introduced in Scotland on 26 March 2006 would dramatically reduce health inequalities in Scotland. England followed Scotland's example in 2007. Recent health statistics (see pages 49 and 56) clearly indicate that Scots are living longer and that the death rates for cancer and heart disease are declining. One would assume that the ban has contributed to this improvement, as Figure 6.2 indicates.

Evidence from researchers at Edinburgh University supports the above assertion. The researchers have been tracking changes in the lifestyle choices of school pupils aged between 11 and 15 every four years since 1990. The latest analysis, published in March 2011, found that between 2006 and 2010 the smoking rates among boys and girls had decreased. The rate for girls had plunged from 28 per cent to 19 per cent by 2010. This suggests that there are roughly 600 fewer 15-year-old smokers across Scotland. Professor Currie, Head of the Research Unit, stated, 'The smoking ban is the most obvious explanation.'

The same report also provided evidence of a decrease in drink and drug use by young people. The number of young people drinking alcohol at least once a week has fallen by more than a third, and experimental and regular cannabis use has halved since 2002.

It was hoped that the smoking ban would act as an incentive for many to quit their smoking habit. It is estimated that the ban could save 600 lives every year and save the NHS £8 million annually. Lung cancer rates are 49 per cent higher in Scotland than in England and Wales and it is clear that advertising campaigns against smoking have had limited impact.

NHS Scotland revealed in September 2011 that the number of Scots giving up smoking had beaten the Scottish Government targets, with 89,075 people quitting in the period 2007–2011.

Some health boards are encouraging pregnant women to stop smoking by offering cash incentives. NHS Tayside has launched an initiative, *Give it up for the baby*, which offers pregnant women £12.50 per week in grocery vouchers if they give up. More than 40 per cent of pregnant women in deprived areas of Tayside smoke during pregnancy. As well as financial incentives, pregnant smokers are being offered nicotine replacement therapy and professional support.

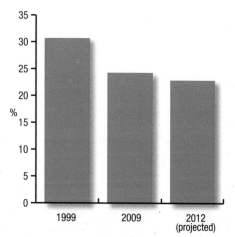

Figure 6.2 Percentage of people in Scotland who smoke ↑

Source: Scottish Household Survey, 2011

Figure 6.3 Cigarette smoking has decreased among Scottish teenagers ↑

Fact File

Do health campaigns work?

Part of the present strategy to improve health is for the Government to spend millions of pounds on television, radio and newspaper campaigns. However, there is ongoing debate over how effective these promotions are at changing people's eating and drinking habits. Do campaigns such as 'Be All You Can Be' improve health?

Evidence from the Department of Health (DoH) in England in May 2011 suggests that the massive cuts made in health promotion budgets, from £93 million under Labour to less than half of that figure, have had dire consequences for many at risk in society. Expenditure on advertising has all but ceased. DoH found that the number of people ringing the drug abuse support helpline, Frank, had fallen by 22 per cent and visits to the Smokefree website had fallen by 50 per cent. Another example is where the Government axed the £1.5 million flu awareness campaign and figures released indicated a rise in deaths from flu from 474 in 2009–10 to 535 in 2010–11.

Diet and obesity

The strategy outlined in *Working Together for a Healthier Scotland* was influenced by the James Report. In 1998 the Labour Government commissioned a committee of experts, under the chairmanship of Professor Philip James, to investigate how to stop children eating junk food. This is food that is rich in sugar, fat and salt, all of which are linked to obesity and heart disease in later life. The main proposal was:

- to introduce healthier food menus in schools
- to stop the sale of sweets, salty snacks and soft drinks inside schools
- to set a legal limit on the age at which children are allowed out of school during lunchtime
- to prohibit food companies targeting food advertising at the young.

For adults, numerous health promotion campaigns have been financed by the Government to raise health awareness. Advertising on the television and radio has had some impact. Many adults are aware that they should try to eat five portions of fruit/vegetables a day and to reduce their salt intake. Campaigns to encourage improved physical fitness, such as 'Be All You Can Be', can be measured in part by the increase in the number of women out jogging and participating in special events.

Figure 6.4 Jamie Oliver ran a highly publicised campaign to improve school dinners ↑

TV chef Jamie Oliver's high-profile campaign to improve school dinners was one factor in influencing government action in England, the cost of which was £220 million. In September 2006 the Labour Government implemented new food standards in England and Wales, following the lead set by the Scottish Government. The Schools (Health Promotion and Nutrition) Scotland Act 2007 and the Nutritional Requirement for Food and Drinks in Schools (Scotland) Regulation 2008 build on the achievement of Hungry for Success by establishing uniform standards for all food and drinks in schools.

Critics of Health Promoting Schools argue that it has had little impact in secondary schools (see below). Secondary pupils are allowed to leave school at lunchtime and may buy fatty foods and fizzy drinks. Professor Annie Anderson, Professor of Health Nutrition at Dundee University, argues that, 'Teenagers are the most challenging group to cater for. It is easy when they are little because they eat in schools, but there is such diversity of competition in secondary with takeaways and vans because pupils can leave school.'

The Child Poverty Action Group is campaigning for free school meals to be introduced to ensure all pupils eat healthy school lunches. From August 2010 all Scottish local authorities can provide free school meals to all Primary 1–3 pupils. In addition, some local councils and schools provide free fruit and breakfast clubs for pupils. However, the significant cuts in local government expenditure threaten the above initiatives.

The Scottish Government can take some comfort from the findings of the September 2010 Scottish Health survey. The survey stated that the number of people classed as overweight had fallen

Case Study: Hungry For Success and Healthy School Meal Scheme, 2002–10

In November 2002, the Scottish Executive launched its £63.5 million initiative to get school children to switch from junk food to healthy eating – 'from stodge to salads'. The campaign introduced nutritional standards for school meals in primary and secondary schools. Food or drinks with a high sugar or salt content were to be phased out, and fresh fruit, vegetables and water were to become recommended food and drink.

In 2004, the Scottish Health Promoting Schools Unit produced the framework document *Being Well – Doing Well*, which provides young people 'with the confidence, skills, knowledge and resilience they will need to make healthier lifestyle choices'.

Pupils and schools were supported by the National Health Promoting Schools website and legislation that dictates how much salt, fat and sugar school meals should contain. By 2006 all primary and secondary schools had a Health Promotion Strategy.

However, a 2010 report by Cordia, the company responsible for Glasgow's school canteens, highlights that tough regulations and legislation on healthy school meals has led to many pupils, especially secondary, rejecting canteen meals in favour of fast-food outlets. Uptake of school meals in Glasgow has plunged from 61 per cent in 2006 to 38 per cent four years later. Fergus Chalmers, chief executive of Cordia, claimed that the rigid regulations have backfired, 'the outcome has been that many school pupils now have an even worse diet due to their desertion of school meals in favour of some of the most unhealthy food'.

for the first time in fifteen years. The proportion of boys with a weight problem fell from 38 per cent to 31 per cent – a significant improvement.

The survey also indicated that children have a healthier diet. In 2003, 54 per cent enjoyed chips at least twice a week but this has dropped to 40 per cent. However, 86 per cent of children were still failing to eat enough fruit and vegetables.

Table 6.1 illustrates the decrease in the number of adults who are clinically obese. This is a group whose health is most at risk, with more women in this category.

Table 6.1 **Percentage of men and women who are obese (BMI 30 or more) in Scotland**

Year	Men (%)	Women (%)
1995	28	36
2003	35	39
2008	36	39
2009	35	38

Source: Scottish Health Survey, 2010

Tackling alcohol abuse

The SNP Government responded to Scotland's alcohol problem by proposing the introduction of a minimum unit pricing (MUP) for alcohol. This proposal was opposed by the other main parties.

The SNP proposed to fix a minimum price for all alcoholic drinks at 45p per unit. That would double or treble the cost of the cheapest super-strength ciders sold by major supermarkets, and raise the cost of cheap supermarket vodka by nearly £4 a bottle.

Nicola Sturgeon, the Scottish Health Secretary, said a minimum price was essential to help tackle the high death toll and health burden from alcohol abuse in Scotland, where 25 per cent more alcohol is drunk per head of population than in the rest of the UK. She claimed that MUP would lead to 50 fewer deaths, 1200 fewer hospital admissions and millions of pounds saved in health care every year.

'For too long, too many Scots have been drinking themselves into an early grave,' she

Case Study: Calorie tax plan recipe for tackling obesity

At a 2011 Public Health Conference attended by the country's leading public health professionals, Dr Chandler, public health doctor for NHS Dumfries and Galloway, proposed that a minimum price per calorie should be set. This proposal would drive up the the cost of fatty and sugary products such as crisps and chocolate.

In Denmark, the Government has already imposed tax increases of 25 per cent on ice cream, chocolate and sweets to tackle the rising tide of obesity and heart disease. Scotland has one of the highest rates of obesity in the developed world.

Dr Chandler argues that it makes no sense for healthier foods to be more expensive than fatty foods. Implementing a minimum price per calorie would ensure that the price of food and drinks would better reflect their nutritional content and calorie density.

said. 'It is no coincidence that as the affordability of alcohol has plummeted in recent decades, alcohol-related deaths, disease, crime and disorder have spiralled. It cannot be right that a man can exceed his weekly recommended alcohol limit for less than £3.50.'

The proposal was supported by Dr Harry Burns, Scotland's chief medical officer, and the British Medical Association in Scotland and at UK level. 'Scotland has an unenviable reputation when it comes to alcohol. We are, sadly, world-class when it comes to damaging our health through heavy drinking,' Burns stated.

The BMA in London said it too supported the measure across the UK. 'There is strong scientific evidence that increasing price reduces rates of alcohol-related problems, particularly among young people,' a BMA spokesman said.

The proposal was lambasted by the drinks industry and opposition politicians at Holyrood. Jackie Baillie, Labour's Shadow Health Secretary at Holyrood, said the proposal was a 'tax on the poor', which would increase revenue for supermarkets by £140 million. 'The SNP have got this one badly wrong. A minimum price of 45p per unit will make no difference to problem drinks, like Buckfast, but it will punish pensioners and people on low incomes,' she said.

In November 2010 the Scottish Parliament rejected the MUP proposal by 76:49 and it was removed from the new Alcohol Bill. The SNP Minority Government failed to convince the other main parties to support minimum pricing. Dr Bruce Ritson, chairperson of the Scottish Health Action on Alcohol Problems, stated, 'We have lost an opportunity to make significant improvements in the health and welfare of the population, particularly those living in the most deprived areas.'

Following its victory in the May 2011 Scottish elections, the new SNP Government promised to reintroduce a minimum pricing Bill.

Figure 6.5 A typical Scottish bar ↑

Case Study: Men's health clinics

One problem associated with innovative health projects funded by the Scottish Executive is that when the money dries up the NHS authorities cannot afford to fund them. Such is the fate of men's health clinics.

Every NHS authority funds well women clinics and in 2002 the Scottish Executive allocated £4 million to run 'well man' health clinics in areas of poor health. In all, sixteen clinics were set up as a result of concern about the lack of interest Scottish men take in their own wellbeing. Ian Anderson, who attended one of the first pilot clinics in Falkirk, claims it changed his life. He has changed his eating and exercise habits and has lost a quarter of his body weight.

It is clear that the clinics have been very successful. An analysis of the first group of men who attended Falkirk clinic revealed that more than 50 per cent had an undiagnosed health problem with nurses' tests picking up cancer, diabetes, heart disease and hypertension.

In June 2006 NHS Greater Glasgow and NHS Lothian stated that their 'well man health clinics would close'. One worker for NHS Greater Glasgow stated, 'I am outraged they have withdrawn funding. Men's health in parts of Glasgow is pretty chronic. Imagine if they said they were going to withdraw well women services. But they withdraw them from men and there's not a peep about it.'

A 2008 University of Aberdeen evaluation highlighted the positive impact of these clinics, especially for those men hardest to reach because of social exclusion. The East Glasgow Men's Health Clinic, for example, was successful in recruiting homeless men by basing its service within the heart of the community.

Activities

1 Outline the health targets set by *Working Together for a Healthier Scotland*.

2 In what ways does the Arbuthnott formula tackle health inequalities?

3 Outline the policies introduced to tackle smoking and obesity and assess their effectiveness.

4 Outline the arguments for and against minimum pricing of alcohol.

Equally Well Report 2008

The SNP Government was aware that the causes of health inequalities were complex and that any strategy had to include a partnership model. The Equally Well Report concentrates on poverty, lack of employment, children's lives and support for families and physical and social environments, as well as on health and wellbeing. Extracts from the report (on the right) clearly indicate that wealth and health inequalities interact. 'There is a clear relationship between income inequality and health inequality' (Scottish Government Minister).

Delivering on the Task Force's recommendations will depend on strong joint working commitment between the NHS, local government, the Third Sector and others within community planning partnerships.

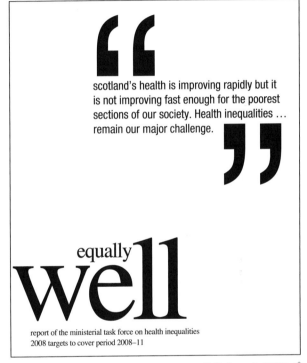

scotland's health is improving rapidly but it is not improving fast enough for the poorest sections of our society. Health inequalities … remain our major challenge.

equally
well

report of the ministerial task force on health inequalities
2008 targets to cover period 2008–11

Figure 6.6 The Scottish Government, Edinburgh 2008 ↑

Key points in the Equally Well Report:

- Health inequalities remain a significant challenge in Scotland.
- The poorest in our society die earlier and have higher rates of disease, including mental illness.
- Tackling health inequalities requires action from national and local government and from other agencies including the NHS, schools, employers and Third Sector.

- Priority areas are children, particularly in the early years, 'killer diseases' such as heart disease, mental health and the harm caused by drugs, alcohol and violence.

Key health inequalities

More babies born to mothers living in the most deprived fifth of areas have a low birth weight than those born to mothers living in the most affluent areas: 9 per cent compared to 5 per cent.

People struggling with poverty and low income have poorer mental health and wellbeing than those with higher incomes or those who find it easy to manage financially.

- In Scotland in 2006, more than two-thirds of the total alcohol-related deaths were in the most deprived two-fifths of areas.
- Those living in the most deprived 10 per cent of areas of Scotland have a suicide risk double that of the Scottish average.
- Adult smoking rates increase with increasing deprivation. In Scotland in 2005–06, smoking rates ranged from 11 per cent in the least deprived 10 per cent of areas to 44 per cent in the most deprived 10 per cent.

In order to reduce inequalities in healthy life expectancy, the Task Force has identified priorities where action is most needed:

- Children's very early years, where inequalities may first arise and influence the rest of people's lives.
- Engaging individuals, families and communities most at risk of poor health in services and decisions relevant to their health.

The Task Force's key recommendations are:

- Keeping 'well health' checks in deprived areas should identify people with depression and anxiety and make sure they get treatment and support.
- The Government should continue to reform the funding of primary care services to meet the needs of groups and communities most at risk of health inequalities.

Characteristics of policies more likely to be effective in reducing inequalities in health:

- **Structural changes in the environment** (e.g. installing affordable heating in damp, cold houses).
- **Legislative and regulatory controls** (e.g. smoking bans in workplaces).
- **Fiscal policies** (e.g. increase price of tobacco and alcohol products).
- **Income support** (e.g. tax and benefit systems, professional welfare rights advice and health care settings).
- **Reducing price barriers** (e.g. free prescriptions).
- **Starting young** (e.g. pre- and post-natal support and interventions, home visiting in infancy, good-quality pre-school day care).

Emphasis to be placed on early intervention

Examples from the Equally Well Report:

- £19 million provided 2007–10 to improve diet and other healthy living activities for pregnant women and children up to age five, in deprived communities.
- The Government's 'Getting it Right for Every Child' (GIRFEC) is about identifying children's needs at any age and bringing together the agencies that should be involved in their lives.
- Health and Wellbeing, literacy and numeracy essential part of Curriculum for Excellence.

- Schools (Health Promotion and Nutrition) – Scotland Act places a duty on local authorities that schools are health promoting.

Decline in children's tooth decay

The Equally Well Report placed emphasis on promoting the health of the young, especially in areas of deprivation. An April 2011 report concluded that tooth decay among young people was at its lowest ever level. The 2005 Action Plan to improve oral health in Scotland set a target for all Primary 1 and Primary 7 children to receive a basic dental inspection at school. Across Scotland 64 per cent of 11-year-olds are decay-free, beating the 2010 target of 60 per cent. Inevitably there is still a gulf between the dental health of children from affluent families and those from poorer homes. The two health boards with the highest rates of tooth decay are Greater Glasgow and Clyde, and Lanarkshire.

Figure 6.7 Preventing child tooth decay ↑

Healthy Child Programme

Children as young as two in Greater Glasgow and Inverclyde are to be subjected to tests including language development to determine their capacity for violent offending, drug

abuse and mental health in later life. Health visitors will screen every child aged between 24 and 30 months for emotional, behavioural and cognitive problems.

Senior health officials hope the Healthy Child Programme will help tackle levels of violent behaviour and drug abuse in Glasgow, which are among the worst in the world. The parents of children identified as at risk will be offered support including parenting classes.

A Swedish study has shown that children aged 30 months who could not put two words together and who had a vocabulary of fewer than 50 words had a 70 per cent probability of having a future psychiatric diagnosis.

Source: Adapted from the *Sunday Times*, 13 March 2011

Free prescriptions in Scotland

In April 2011 all prescriptions became free in Scotland and this flagship policy of the SNP Government was hailed as a significant strategy in improving the health of the Scottish public and in reducing health inequalities. Critics argued that in a time of economic recession it was a misguided policy that would deprive the NHS of badly needed funding and would benefit the better off (see Figure 6.11 on page 71).

Obviously it is too early to assess the impact of the abolition of charges on the wealth of the Scottish public. However, evidence from Wales suggests that it has had a beneficial impact on health. Wales completely abolished fees in 2007 after a phased reduction since 2004. In an official 2010 Welsh report, *Helping to Improve Wales'*

Health: Free Prescriptions Three Years On, Edwina Hart, Minister for Health and Social Services stated, 'The abolition of prescriptions charges is one of the major achievements of the Welsh Assembly Government.'

The Welsh Report argues that the introduction of free prescriptions has made access to medicines fairer for all and has not led to a massive increase in the number of prescriptions dispensed. Free prescription also does away with bureaucracy as it is no longer means tested. The cost of checking eligibility and countering fraud activities, which included payment to pharmacists, was £0.83 million a year. The Scottish Government estimates that it will save more than £1 million.

Fact File

In Scotland and Wales prescription charges are free. In England a prescription charge is £7.40. It is free in England for all of those who are:

- claiming Income Support
- claiming income-based Jobseeker's Allowance
- claiming income-related Employment and Support Allowance
- 60 or over or are under 16
- pregnant or have had a baby in the last twelve months
- suffering from a medical condition that is listed on the free prescription list.

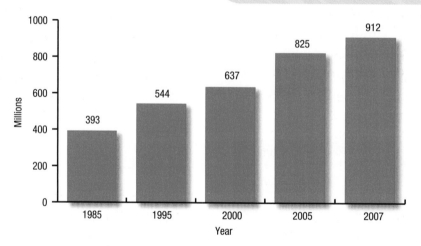

Figure 6.8 Prescriptions (millions) UK ↑

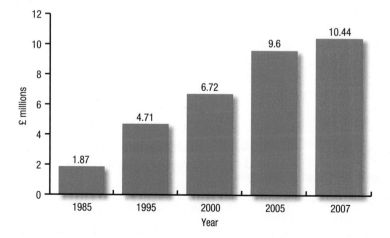

Figure 6.9 Total costs for prescriptions (millions) UK ↑

'Prescription charges are a tax on ill health, and can be a barrier to good health for too many people. This Scottish Government is committed to building a healthier nation; through tackling the health inequalities that still scar our nation and supporting people to live longer and lead healthier lives. I also want the NHS to be true to its founding principle: the principle of health care free at the point of need.'

Figure 6.10 Nicola Sturgeon, Deputy First Minister and Cabinet Secretary for Health and Wellbeing and Cities Strategy ↑

Source: Scottish Parliament, 2008

Arguments in favour of free prescriptions	Arguments against free prescriptions
1 Meets the founding principles of the NHS of health care free at the point of need. Prescription charges are a tax on ill health. Wales introduced free prescriptions in 2007. The present system is inconsistent, for example, those patients with epilepsy receive free prescriptions while those with high blood pressure or Parkinson's disease have to pay.	1 The principles of free prescriptions were quickly abandoned in the 1950s. We have free visits to the doctor and hospital treatment is free. It will encourage people to obtain prescriptions that they do not need. Prescription charges still exist in England.
2 It will make a significant contribution to achieving a healthier Scotland. No longer will cost discourage the sick from consulting their doctor and picking up their prescriptions. Those working individuals just above the Income Support level are facing the present hardships of the economic recession. Many will receive no wage rises in the period 2011–13 and will face a reduction in their living standards.	2 There is no evidence that it will reduce health inequalities. The elderly and those on Income Support do not pay at present. The massive cuts in public expenditure in the period 2011–14 suggest that we cannot afford free prescriptions.
3 In the long run it will save money. It will improve people's health and place less pressure on the NHS. Free drugs to control blood pressure and heart problems will reduce morbidity and mortality figures. Free prescriptions will only reduce the income received by the NHS by £57 million annually.	3 Real cuts are being made in the NHS budget and we cannot afford to lose £57 million of income every year. The money is needed to employ more nurses and to provide better care.

Figure 6.11 The arguments in favour of and against free prescriptions ↑

Prior to April 2011:

- In Scotland 50 per cent of the population qualified for free prescriptions. Around 92 per cent of all prescriptions (68 million) were supplied to patients free of charge.
- The loss of income from prescription charges is estimated at £57 million.

In September 2011:

- NHS Scotland reported that almost half a million Scots take anti-depressants.

Role of the private sector within the NHS

The practice of patients 'going private' and paying for the services of GPs, consultants and hospital provision is long standing within the UK. Roughly 13 per cent of the UK population is covered by private health insurance. The private sector was regarded as a factor in health inequalities with, for example, those covered by private health being able to jump the queue for operations.

The role of the private sector working in partnership with the NHS to tackle health inequalities creates great controversy. On the one hand, opponents of the private sector claim that such partnerships will destroy state-funded health care provision and this creeping privatisation will eventually create a USA-style model of a first-class private sector and a third-rate state system dealing with trauma and acute illness. Supporters of the involvement of the private sector argue that partnership models reduce waiting lists, improve efficiency and provide state-of-the-art hospitals (see Creeping privatisation, right).

The Conservative Party under Margaret Thatcher had involved the private sector in the delivery of the NHS, a move that was opposed

Creeping privatisation

The term 'privatisation' covers a range of NHS services provided by the private sector:

- the practice of contracting services out to the private sector (competitive tendering), for example ancillary services, namely laundry, cleaning and catering being provided by a private firm
- the practice of buying services from the private sector, for example the hiring of medical equipment or operations on NHS patients by the private sector
- Public Private Partnership Programmes (PPPP) whereby private firms build and run NHS hospitals. This had been a Conservative programme, Private Finance Initiative, which was opposed by Labour. However, when Labour came to power in 1997 they changed the name to PPPP and accelerated the number of state-of-the art hospitals being built by the private sector. This programme has been especially controversial. In the short term, PPPP is an excellent initiative as it provides brand-new modern hospitals for patients and staff, to replace Victorian institutions. However, critics would argue that it is not value for money and that the private sector is making massive profits through charges for services and interest charges.

This 'buy now, pay later' policy adds further pressure to NHS spending, which faces cuts in its future spending. The NHS in Scotland faces an estimated massive bill of £6.7 billion in repayments over the next 30 years. The 27 capital projects, for example Hairmyres Hospital in East Kilbride, covered by the £6.7 billion have an estimated value of the much smaller sum of £1.28 billion. The SNP Government is hostile to PPPP and refers to the scandal of the PPPP-built Royal Infirmary of Edinburgh where, overall, £1.5 billion will be paid for the £228 million it cost to build.

by Labour. The UK Labour Governments, once hostile to private health care, embraced the private sector in the period 1997–2010. In 2000 Labour redefined the core principles of the NHS to include partnership with the private sector. The new Conservative/Liberal Democrat Coalition Government has been accused of wishing to introduce further privatisation with its plans to abolish NHS management bureaucracy and to transfer more than 65 per cent of the £110 billion NHS England budget to consortiums of GPs. These consortiums will buy the hospital treatment and drugs their patients need either from the NHS or from private providers. Again these consortiums can employ the private sector to administer their activities.

In August 2011 a private health firm, Circle Health Care, took over the running of Hinchingbrooke Hospital in Cambridgeshire. This was the first time that a major hospital within the NHS system would be wholly managed by a private firm.

If the above reforms go through then the differences between Scotland and England will further widen (see Differences between Scotland and England, right). During a BBC Question Time programme in April 2011, Scottish First Minister Alex Salmond accused all three parties in England of supporting the privatisation of the

NHS and stated that Scotland would remain true to the original principles of the NHS.

Differences between Scotland and England

- A single NHS system in Scotland – no NHS trust hospitals.

- No foundation hospitals – recent health reforms in England have reintroduced the internal market.

- Free eye tests and prescriptions in Scotland.

- The proportion of jobs in the public sector in Scotland is 24 per cent, whereas in England it is 20 per cent.

- Significantly less involvement of the private sector; target in England is to increase private sector delivery of operations from 8 per cent to 15 per cent.

- Free personal care in Scotland for elderly people who require it.

- There is still more per capita health spending in Scotland – England, though, is catching up.

- There are still more doctors, nurses and hospital beds in Scotland than in England. Based on population, Scotland has 23 per cent more hospital doctors, 30 per cent more nurses and family doctors.

- In Scotland there are no university tuition fees. In England fees vary from £3290 to £9000 from 2012.

Figure 6.12 The Royal Infirmary of Edinburgh, a PPPP hospital ↑

Improved health

Both the UK and Scottish Governments in the period 1997 to 2011 set out to improve the health of British citizens and to reduce health and wealth inequalities. These were the golden years of plenty and we have now entered the age of austerity where cuts are being made to public services and unemployment is increasing, which will impact on the health of UK citizens.

The health of all citizens is improving, including those in areas of deprivation. As indicated in Table 5.3 on page 49, the life expectancy of men who live in Glasgow has increased by 2.6 years, which is excellent news. However, the health gap between affluent and poorer areas has widened. The gap in male life expectancy between East Dunbartonshire and Glasgow has risen from 6.3 years in 1997 to 7.3 years in 2007.

It is clear that the ban on smoking in public places has improved the health of the nation. According to the 2010 Scottish Household Survey, more than 200,000 Scots have given up smoking over the last ten years.

Table 6.2 clearly highlights that death rates from coronary heart disease have significantly fallen across the UK, especially for women. The Scottish rate is disappointing compared to the rest of the UK; so much has still to be done in the future with fewer resources to improve the health of the Scottish people and to reduce health inequalities.

Activities

1 Outline the key points of Equally Well and its main recommendations.

2 To what extent has the oral health of children improved?

3 Outline the arguments for and against free prescriptions.

4 Describe the types of activities that would be covered by the term 'privatisation'.

5 To what extent does the private sector help to improve health?

Essay question

Assess the effectiveness of government policies to reduce health inequalities.

Table 6.2 **Decrease in death rate from coronary heart disease in men and women under 65, 2003–09, UK and Europe**

	Men (%)	Women (%)
UK	24	31
England	25	32
Scotland	15	26
Wales	26	33
Northern Ireland	19	26
Netherlands	31	38
Finland	17	22
European Union	14	17

Source: British Health Foundation, 2011

Gender and Ethnicity: Social and Economic Inequalities

Two groups of people who face particular social and economic inequalities are women and ethnic minorities (health issues are discussed in Chapter 5). These groups are affected by inequalities caused by social class, the economic climate and government policy, but they face the added dimensions of discrimination, stereotyping and biology.

Social change

Society is changing. People's living arrangements changed significantly in the last quarter of the twentieth century. Currently around 50 per cent of men and women live as married couples. One in ten men and women now cohabit. More than 20 per cent of women and nearly 30 per cent of men live on their own and never marry. There are more than three times as many widows as widowers because women tend to live longer.

Since 1971, the proportion of the population living in 'traditional' family households with married parents and children has fallen from 52 per cent to 37 per cent. Nearly 25 per cent of children live in lone-parent households. Of these, 93 per cent are headed by lone mothers.

Women's changing economic role

In the twentieth century dramatic changes took place in the economic and social position of women in UK society. But, despite these changes, women have yet to achieve equality.

In 2010 there were almost the same number of men and women in jobs – 12.6 million men and 12.2 million women. However, almost half of the female jobs were part time (5.2 million) compared to 1.5 million for men.

Women make an increasingly important contribution to the income of families with children. Women in lone-parent families are obviously the only breadwinner. In two-parent families the woman's economic contribution is

Fact File

Why are women more likely to suffer from poverty?

Women earn less
- lower pay for the same work
- women work in lower-paid sectors of the economy
- interrupted employment
- part-time work
- glass ceiling.

Women take greater responsibility for family and caring
- lone parents
- greater burden for the cost of children
- women's traditional role as carer.

Women live longer and are poorer than men and more women depend on welfare benefits.

often the difference between living in poverty or not. In families where both parents work, even if one only works part time, 4 per cent had incomes in the bottom 20 per cent of incomes. When only one parent works 17 per cent are in the bottom 20 per cent.

On average women have lower incomes than men. They work in lower-paid sectors of the economy, are less likely to reach the top in their chosen careers and are more likely to work in part-time jobs or depend on benefits because they are lone parents.

Women continue to be placed in the traditional role as carer for children, elderly, sick and disabled relatives. This places them at a financial disadvantage because they take career breaks or work part time or live on welfare. In addition the extra costs of funding those who need to be cared for are costs that women share so they have less to spend on themselves. Even in two-parent relationships, women bear a greater burden of the cost of children.

Finally, women live longer. A life lived in poverty continues beyond retirement age. There are more elderly women than men in the UK and many more women depend on means-tested benefits because they did not have careers that enabled them to earn the right to a pension. There are three times as many single female pensioners as there are males and more live on lower incomes.

Women earn less

The best-paid women who work full time earn around 20 per cent less than the best-paid men who work full time, the same difference as a decade ago. There is still a gap between low-paid male and female earnings for full-time employees, but this gap has narrowed over the last decade.

Pay differentials vary by region. Pay inequalities for full-time employees are greater in London and the South East than elsewhere, with the differences being particularly great in inner London.

The gender pay gap also varies from industry to industry with the biggest differential being in banking and finance where men earn 44 per cent more than women. In health and social work men earn 30 per cent more, in hotels and restaurants it is 13 per cent more and even in education it is 11 per cent more. The smallest difference is in agriculture and forestry where men earn 2 per cent more than women.

Research by the Women and Equality Unit indicated that the main reason for lower earnings was discrimination, followed by fewer women working in full-time employment, interruptions to working lives and careers caused by family care commitments, and then working in lower-paid sectors of the economy. Also the *Dimensions of Diversity Report* from NHS Scotland (2010) says, 'Early sexual activity that results in birth can be detrimental to longer-term life chances for young women, disrupting potential educational and employment opportunities.'

Discrimination – lower pay for the same work

Gender pay differentials still remain. For example, the median hourly earnings of full-time female medical practitioners are 23 per cent less than male earnings. Female legal professionals earn 21 per cent less, and female accountants earn 15 per cent less.

Men start to earn more as soon as they enter the job market and the gender earnings gap widens with age. Women aged 18–21 earn 2 per cent less than men but those aged 40–49 earn 20 per cent less.

Recent research indicates that education and experience is equal between men and women at the outset of their careers so the gender pay gap is small. However, after ten years in the job market, despite working continuously full time, a

Figure 7.1 Women make up 59 per cent of the catering workforce ↑

woman's income is 12 per cent less than a man's. Part of the difference may be explained by men and women entering different occupations, but the major cause is discrimination.

Women work in lower-paid sectors of the economy

Men and women work in different areas of the economy and within these in different occupations. Women are over-represented in areas of the economy that are low paid. Nearly two-thirds of women are employed in twelve occupation groups. These are sometime described as the five 'c's – caring, cashiering, catering, cleaning and clerical occupations.

Of those working in education, social work and health services 78.3 per cent are women and they are also well represented in offices dealing with cash, marketing and sales, and personnel. These sectors have been traditionally lower paid than equivalent skilled work in other areas of the economy.

More than twice as many men as women are in the higher and professional occupations in the UK. Therefore in occupations where women are over-represented men tend to have the higher managerial positions.

Since 2000 women have experienced some improvement because of structural changes in the economy. The service sector is growing. Women's numbers are growing in occupations previously dominated by men. Females now account for 75 per cent of pharmacists, 33 per cent of medical practitioners, nearly half of all lawyers and almost 40 per cent of all accountants. The proportion of female managers and senior officials increased from less than 10 per cent in the early 1990s to one-third in 2005. Therefore increasing numbers of women are entering occupations that offer higher earnings.

However, even in the new industries there are several areas where women are poorly represented. Women account for only 14 per cent of the professionals in science and technology and the number of female professionals in information and communications technology is falling.

Interrupted employment

Women are more likely than men to take time out of work to care for children or other people. Therefore their working lives are interrupted over time. Experience is one of the factors that employers reward and it is often difficult for women to return to work at the same level or at a higher level after taking time out.

After a long period out of work women face barriers to returning such as low confidence and outdated skills. Even after a relatively short time it can be difficult for women to find jobs that match their skills, particularly if the work they want to find is local or part time.

A low-skilled mother of two taking time out to care for her children loses £250,000 in earnings over her lifetime. An interrupted employment record means fewer pension contributions so women continue to face reduced circumstances when they are old.

Part-time work

Many more women than men work part time. Women are most likely to work part time when they are caring for young children. Approximately two-thirds of women with children under the age of eleven work part time, compared to only one-third of women with no dependent children.

Women tend to work part time between the ages of 25 and 45. This is the main child-rearing age but they are also the prime years of their career. Men, on the other hand, mostly work part time when they are students or winding down to retirement. Research has shown that a woman who worked part time for just one year during the prime of her career can expect to earn 10 per cent less than a woman who never worked part time.

Women who work part time earn 32 per cent less per hour than women who work full time and 41 per cent less than men who work full time. Part of the reason is that women working part time often have lower levels of education than those who work full time. However, the main reason is that part-time work is concentrated in lower-paid jobs. One in four women working part time will be employed as retail sales assistants, cleaners or care assistants. Few work as managers.

In order to find work at times that suit their child care responsibilities many women have to change their employer and their occupation and take a pay cut.

Time travelling to and from work is also an issue. Women with children often need to have shorter travel-to-work times because they also have to access child care. Or they can only travel a short distance because they have to fit work and travel into the time when their children are at school or nursery. This limits the range of jobs available to them.

The glass ceiling

The term 'glass ceiling' was first used in the 1980s to describe the invisible barrier that stops women (and other disadvantaged groups)

reaching the top in their chosen career. It is usually applied to barriers to senior management positions.

The glass ceiling is created in a number of informal ways:

- Women as the main carers take career breaks, which prevent career development.
- It is difficult for women to access male-dominated networks based on after-hours socialising in the pub and at the golf club, which influence appointments and promotion.
- 'Presenteeism' is an idea that senior management must be seen to be working long hours. There is a lack of part-time work and flexible working at senior levels.
- Stereotyping and discrimination. Male directors may develop prejudices about a woman's commitment and ambitions – in particular, having children is seen to be incompatible with senior roles.
- Lack of role models. There are few female role models in senior positions to dispel these stereotypes and to inspire women into senior levels.

Table 7.1 shows that women are very much in the minority in top posts in the UK. Barely one-third of all managers and senior officials are women and they tend to be in the lower-paid areas of management. For example, 60 per cent of personnel and marketing managers whose median pay is less than £19 per hour are women, but only 26 per cent of corporate managers and senior officials, whose median pay is more than £39 per hour, are women (see Female doctors are denied NHS top jobs on page 80).

According to women the main barrier preventing them taking on senior roles is the lack of quality part-time work. The prevailing male belief in 'presenteeism' at the top levels of business prevents this. Yet there are some

Table 7.1 **Percentage of women in top posts in the UK, 2003 and 2007**

	2003	2007
MPs	18.1	19.5
Cabinet	23.8	34.8
MSPs	39.5	38.8
Directors in FTSE 100 companies	8.6	10.4
Public appointments	35.7	35.5
Local authority chief executives	13.1	20.6
Senior ranks armed forces	0.6	0.4
Senior police officers	7.6	12.3
Senior judges	6.8	9.8
Civil service top management	22.9	26.3
Chief executives of voluntary organisations	45.2	46.0
Head teachers of secondary schools	30.1	n/a

Source: EOC – Sex and Power: Who Runs Britain? 2007

companies that are beginning to make changes and have seen benefits.

MSN UK (Microsoft) introduced a project to move away from long hours and presenteeism when it opened up flexible working for all staff. It began by retraining its senior managers. The business has benefited from improved morale and staff retention and 81 per cent of staff believe they provide a better service and meet their objectives because they work flexibly.

However, some academics are challenging the view that discrimination still exists. Catherine Hakim, a university academic, argues that the pay gap is down to women's lifestyle choice – the battle for sexual equality is over. In a 2011 report she claims that women now have the freedom to choose between raising children and entering senior posts and that the new 2010 Equality Law is pointless and based on feminist myths. In the reports she says, 'People are confusing

equal opportunities with equal outcomes, and there is little support for social engineering being demanded by feminists and legislators.'

Catherine Hakim also argues that a top-flight career is not the priority for many women and that previous equality legislation has not failed. A person in a CEO (chief executive) post is expected to work long hours and have almost total commitment to a career.

A 2010 government review highlighted that only five chief executives of FTSE 100 companies are women and only 13 per cent of these firms' boards of directors are female. More than half of Britain's 250 biggest public companies have no female directors.

Critics of Hakim argue that these figures explain why further action is needed to break the glass ceiling. They support positive discrimination action, such as suggestions that 40 per cent of the company board should be female.

Figure 7.2 Women are underrepresented among consultants ↑

Female doctors are denied NHS top jobs

The NHS faces a chronic shortage of women in senior positions as female medical staff hit a glass ceiling, doctors' leaders are warning.

Fewer than 30 per cent of consultant posts in the health service are held by women, even though two-thirds of doctors entering the profession are female. Women doctors also earn, in general, 18 per cent less than male doctors.

Now the British Medical Association (BMA) – which represents more than 140,000 doctors and medical students – is launching a new initiative called Women In Medicine to try to boost the number of women in senior medical posts.

Professor Bhupinder Sandhu, the chair of the BMA's equality and diversity committee, said, 'While equality between male and female doctors is relatively okay at the bottom end of the profession, for example getting into medical school and the early jobs in medicine, there are still areas where women are not rising to senior positions.

Part of the problem is the need for flexible working, but that is much easier now – particularly in the NHS where most doctors work. The other problem is that women are not pushing themselves forward.'

While women account for up to 59 per cent of the medical workforce, they account for just 28 per cent of consultants.

The glass ceiling is even more marked in universities, where only 11 per cent of professors and 36 per cent of lecturers are women.

Around 45 per cent of BMA members are women. However, the number of women taking up positions on its committees is 30 per cent (up from 19 per cent in 2002–03).

Source: Extract from 'Female doctors fail to break through the glass ceiling', Rachel Ellis, *Observer*, 22 August 2010

The significant increase in the number of women graduates (see Figure 7.3) explains why women are now earning more than men until the age of 30, as indicated in Table 7.2. However, a significant gap opens especially in the 40–49 age group.

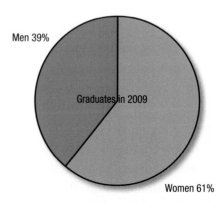

Men 39%

Graduates in 2009

Women 61%

Figure 7.3 In 2009, 61 per cent of graduates were women and 39 per cent were men ↑

Table 7.2 **Pay gap – women earn more than men until the age of 30**

Women	Age	Men
+ 2.1%	22–29	
	30–39	+ 2.9%
	40–49	+ 16.1%
	50–59	+ 9.6%

Source: Equality and Human Rights wage audit, 2010

The number of women who are starting up their own companies is on the increase. There are now 44 women for every 100 men starting their own enterprises and the gap narrows every year. Women are choosing to give up guaranteed salaries, bonuses, pensions, health insurance, and so on, for the risk, hard work and uncertainty of their own enterprise. However, according to the Edinburgh's Businesswomen's Club, female-owned businesses make up just 18 per cent of the 300,000 registered businesses – the UK average is about 30 per cent. The benefit is the opportunity to work flexibly. A 2011 City report reveals that the number of female multi-millionaires has increased by 40 per cent since 2005. The report calculates that there are 72,000 women in the UK with liquid assets of more than £2.5 million. Scottish women include Michelle Mone, the Ultimo tycoon, and Ann Gloag, the Perth-born co-founder of the Stagecoach travel empire.

Therefore the idea that women do not get promotion in established companies because they do not have enough drive is not correct or women would not be taking risks to start their own businesses. The failure of established businesses to promote women is for reasons other than ability and ambition.

In primary schools, 82 per cent of teachers are women yet nearly half of primary heads are men. In secondary teaching, women account for nearly half of the teachers but only 30 per cent are head teachers. Women now account for 60 per cent of university undergraduates, yet in higher education they account for only 40 per cent of academics and just 30 per cent are department heads. Women are more likely to be offered fixed-term contracts rather than a staff job – 48 per cent of women are on fixed-term contracts compared to 38 per cent of men. Only 13 per cent of professors in older universities are women.

Figure 7.4 **Michelle Mone. OBE** ↑

Table 7.3 **Percentage of school leavers with Highers in selected subjects by gender, 2009**

	Girls (%)	Boys (%)
English	60	40
Mathematics	48	52
Biology	66	34
Modern Studies	64	36
History	57	43
Chemistry	48	52
Geography	53	47
Business Management	58	42
Physics	29	71

Source: Scottish Executive (2010) SQA attainment and school leaver qualifications in Scotland, 2008–09

According to the Equal Opportunities Commission (EOC), at the current rate of progress it will take women another 20 years before they gain equality in civil servant top management; 40 years for equality as top judges; 60 years for equality as female directors of FTSE 100 companies; and 200 years or 40 elections to get equality of MPs in the UK Parliament.

Females have overtaken males in education qualifications. Overall girls leave school with better qualifications than boys. In 2009, 23.4 per cent of S6 girls left school with five or more Highers while only 17.8 per cent boys were as successful.

As stated above, more girls are now going on to university and higher education than boys. Females now outperform males at both undergraduate and postgraduate levels. Around 60 per cent of higher education qualifications are obtained by women.

The subjects boys and girls choose will influence their careers. At A level, girls are well represented in subjects such as English, psychology, art and design, sociology, biology and the expressive arts/drama, while boys tend to choose physics, mathematics, economics, computing and business studies. Similarly in Scotland, girls choose different subjects to boys.

More women than men study social science subjects such as history, and arts subjects such as languages. These generally lead to less well-paid sectors of the economy. On the other hand nearly 70 per cent of students of medicine and dentistry are women.

However, even where men and women enter the same occupation with the same qualifications there can be a salary gap. Therefore in many areas of life women are still faced with obstacles to advancement and promotion in their chosen career.

Activities

1 How has social and economic change over the last 30 years affected the role of women?

2 To what extent do women earn less than men?

3 The gender pay gap is not constant over a woman's lifetime. Explain this.

4 To what extent do the following factors reduce the economic status of women:
   - type of employment
   - career breaks
   - part-time working?

5 The glass ceiling remains the most significant barrier to women in employment. Discuss.

Women take greater responsibility for family and caring

Lone parents

In the UK 25 per cent of families are lone-parent families – 1.7 million parents with 2.9 million dependent children. Nine out of ten lone parents are lone mothers. In Scotland there are 162,000 lone-parent families with more than 280,000 children.

Approximately 10 per cent of lone parents are under 25 whereas 55 per cent are in the age group 25–44. Most become lone parents through separation and divorce, so most lone parents are over 25.

Lone-parent families are particularly vulnerable to poverty. In Scotland 70 per cent of lone-parent families have an income of less than £10,000 per year compared to only 25 per cent of two-parent families. Figures show that 79 per cent of lone parents have no savings compared to 41 per cent of two-parent families.

The employment rate for lone parents is much lower than for mothers who are married or cohabiting. The reason for the difference is child care. Where there are two parents, one can be looking after the family while the other is out at work.

In Sweden 70 per cent of lone mothers work and in France the figure is 82 per cent, whereas in the UK it is 55 per cent. In France and Sweden there is far more affordable child care available for lone parents. In the UK the Childcare Cost Survey for the Day Care Trust found that a full-time nursery place for a child under two typically costs more than £7000 per year. It found that 90 per cent of lone parents say they would like to find paid employment but face barriers. They identify the main one as the cost and availability of child care.

Another problem is that many lone parents have limited qualifications or skills. A survey for the Department of Social Security reported that 50 per cent of lone parents had no educational qualifications, compared with 38 per cent of all women aged 25–49.

When lone parents find work it is often low paid so they merely replace workless poverty with working poverty. Therefore lone parents have a high risk of living in poverty whether they are in work or not.

The lack of income has an impact on living standards and health. Children in lone-parent families are much more likely to go without necessities than children in two-parent families. In housing, lone parents in Scotland are more dependent on rented housing and are more likely to live in a flat. Only 25 per cent of lone parents live in owner-occupied housing compared to 71 per cent of two-parent families.

Whatever the structure of the family, women tend to bear a greater burden of the cost of bringing up children than men. Women experience poverty in different ways from men because the responsibility for managing household poverty usually falls on the women.

Figure 7.5 Lone mothers face many problems ↑

The majority of women see the wellbeing of their children as their major family priority. It often means that debt management becomes a daily as well as a long-term problem for women. Debt is often necessary to even out spending over a period of time but it is kept hidden from their partners.

Women who have children tend to drop out of the labour market, but those who remain in work continue to bear the main responsibility for child care and domestic work. The *UK Time Use Survey* undertaken by the Equal Opportunities Commission found that mothers did 75 per cent of child care through the week and two-thirds at the weekend. This amounted to two hours each weekday and one-and-a-half hours each Saturday and Sunday. Fathers did around 45 minutes as a daily average through the week and nearly one hour at the weekend.

Women are also more likely than men to be carers for elderly or disabled relatives and friends. Almost 6 million people, 11 per cent of the population, provide unpaid care. The proportion of unpaid carers increases as women get older.

Women with these caring responsibilities are much more likely than men to work part time or not at all whereas the majority of men with caring responsibilities who do paid work have full-time jobs. This means that women are more likely to have to survive on reduced incomes throughout their lives. At times when they could be earning and contributing to pension rights they are unable do so because of the caring role they adopt or are expected to adopt. Ultimately this means they will continue to live in poverty past retirement age.

Women are more dependent on welfare benefits

There are 26 per cent more women than men over the age of 60. For those aged over 80 there are double the number of women. Life expectancy for the UK is 77.3 years for men and 81.5 years for women. In Scotland it is lower at 75.4 for men and 80.1 for women.

As working age women on average have lower incomes they make fewer contributions and so have fewer pension rights. More than 80 per cent of women who retire are not entitled to a full basic State Pension based on their own contributions. Recent research estimates that women who do not have children and who have middle-ranked skills earn £250,000 less over their lifetime than similarly skilled men. For women who have children the difference is much greater.

Women are less likely to have a pension than a man and part-time female workers are the least likely group to gain access to a pension. Approximately 66 per cent of male full-time employees had an occupational or private pension whereas 63 per cent of full-time female workers and only 41 per cent of part-time female workers had a pension. Lower-paid jobs are less likely to have occupational pension schemes. As women are over-represented in these jobs they are less likely to retire with a decent pension and so have to rely on means-tested benefits.

As a result 44 per cent of single female pensioners depend solely on the State Pension and have to seek Pension Credits compared to only 28 per cent of single male pensioners. More male pensioners have occupational and personal pensions.

Access to the State Pension is to be later for both men and women but will particularly affect women. Currently the pensionable age is rising for women so that by 2020 both men and women will access their pension only when they reach the age of 66. Then the plan is to increase both pensionable ages to 68 by 2046. These age increases will also affect other benefits linked to age such as Winter Fuel Payment, Pension Credit, etc. A woman born in January 1950 would receive her State Pension in January 2010; in contrast a woman born in January 1954 will need to wait until 2017 before she receives her State Pension.

In conclusion, women live longer and live poorer than men. Throughout their working lives they are paid less for comparable work, they are more likely to work in low-paid employment, work part time and have long periods when they do not work and may have to live on benefits. With separation, divorce and cohabitation becoming increasingly common, women can no longer depend on husbands or partners to provide for them in their old age. Consequently far more women face poverty throughout their working lives and for longer in their retirement years because they live longer than men.

Activities

1   Assess the impact of lone parenthood on women in Scotland and the UK.

2   Critically examine the view that women in families are far more likely to suffer poverty.

Race and ethnic inequalities

Black and Minority Ethnic (BME) is commonly used by organisations such as the Equality and Human Rights Commission (EHRC) when speaking of ethnic minorities. The BME population is about 8 per cent of the total UK population. It has risen from 3 million in 1991 to almost 5 million today. In Scotland the minority population is 2 per cent of the total population. The BME community consists of a variety of groups each of which has different experiences of wealth and poverty. In Scotland the largest groups are Pakistani (31%), Chinese (16%), Indian (15%) and Mixed Background (13%). Bangladeshis count for only 2 per cent of the ethnic minority population in Scotland and Black African (5%) and Caribbean (2%) are small groups compared to their size in England.

Minority ethnic groups have a younger age profile than White Scots with more aged under 35 and fewer aged over 55. For example, 50 per cent of Pakistanis are under 25 compared to 32 per cent of the white population. This will have an effect when trying to compare the health profiles of different communities.

Table 7.4 **Risk of being on low income by group**

Group	%
White	18
Mixed	33
Indian	30
Pakistani/Bangladeshi	52
Black Caribbean	25
Black non-Caribbean	45
Chinese or other ethnic group	36

Source: Department for Work and Pensions (DWP)

A higher proportion of Bangladeshis, Pakistanis and the Black non-Caribbean groups are living in poverty than any other groups.

Reasons for poverty in the BME communities:

- lower income
- culture
- higher unemployment
- discrimination.

Lower income

With the exception of the Indian group, most minority groups earn less than the White British group. In the past many migrants had lower qualifications or qualifications not recognised in the UK, so many were concentrated in low-pay industries such as hotels and catering.

Income inequalities vary by group and gender. While black males earn considerably less than white males, black females earn considerably more than white females. Many white females work part time while more black females work full time. Both Indian males and females earn more than their white counterparts because they have higher levels of qualifications.

In Scotland, the ethnic groups living in poverty vary slightly from the UK pattern. There are significantly fewer Indians and Chinese in the bottom 40 per cent of deprivation. Only 29 per cent of Indians and 30 per cent of Chinese compared to 42 per cent of White Scots live in deprivation, whereas 48 per cent of Pakistanis and 49 per cent of Bangladeshis are in this category.

Culture

Reasons for inequalities are also cultural. In some groups there is less religious or family pressure to retain the two-parent family unit. Black Africans and Black Caribbeans and those in the Mixed group have a higher proportion of lone-parent families. Therefore many have to live on benefits

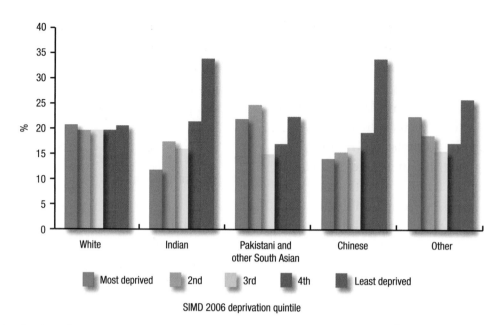

Figure 7.6 Distribution of population by ethnic group and deprivation, Scotland 2001

Source: Dimensions of Diversity Report, NHS Scotland, 2010

or take low-paid employment, so they and their families live in poverty.

On the other hand, the poorest groups, Pakistanis and Bangladeshis, are more likely to be married. Pakistani and Bangladeshi women are mainly Muslim and the cultural expectation is for them to stay at home and look after larger families. Three-quarters of Bangladeshi women and more than two-thirds of Pakistani women are economically inactive.

The Pakistani and Bangladeshi female populations are relatively young and have a larger proportion of women of child-bearing age. Roughly 74 per cent of Bangladeshi households and 66 per cent of Pakistani households have dependent children, figures that are much greater than Indian (50%) and Black African (48%) households. Only 28 per cent of White British households have dependent children. On average the size of a Pakistani family is 3.4 children and for Bangladeshis it is 3.6, significantly larger than 2.1 for White women of child-bearing age.

Another reason why many Pakistani and Bangladeshi women stay at home is that they do not have the skills needed to work and in many

cases their English is poor, which is a major barrier to finding employment.

Higher unemployment

BME groups have always faced higher rates of unemployment than White British. All groups except the Indian group suffer between two and three times the level of unemployment than the majority population. Indian men have the lowest unemployment rates among the ethnic minority groups and rates are only marginally higher than those for White British men.

First generation migrants to the UK face several disadvantages that lead to higher unemployment such as language difficulties, a lack of recognised qualifications and racial prejudice. Some groups are affected by local economic circumstances because they are concentrated in these areas. For example, the Pakistani community, which is concentrated in the North and Midlands of England, was badly affected by the closure of manufacturing industries in these areas.

Variations in the unemployment rate may also be a reflection of different skills and qualifications that each ethnic group possesses. Indian men have low unemployment rates – around 30 per cent of them have degree level qualifications whereas relatively few, 15 per cent, have no qualifications. Pakistani and Bangladeshi men have high rates of unemployment. Only 11 per cent and 15 per cent respectively have degree level qualifications whereas 29 per cent and 40 per cent respectively have no qualifications.

Figure 7.7 An Asian family in the UK ↑

Figure 7.8 illustrates the patchy progress in the number of BMEs who are self-employed. While there has been a significant increase in the number of Pakistani and Black Caribbean self-employed men, the Chinese and Indian figures have declined.

In the last ten years all ethnic groups have improved their education attainment. GCSE results in England show Indian and Chinese boys and girls gaining more passes than candidates from the White British ethnic group. These improvements are mirrored at degree level. The proportion of Chinese, Indian and Black Africans achieving a degree is now significantly higher than for the White British ethnic group.

Discrimination

Race discrimination in the UK takes three forms: direct discrimination, indirect discrimination and institutional discrimination.

Direct discrimination is when a group of people is treated less favourably on the grounds

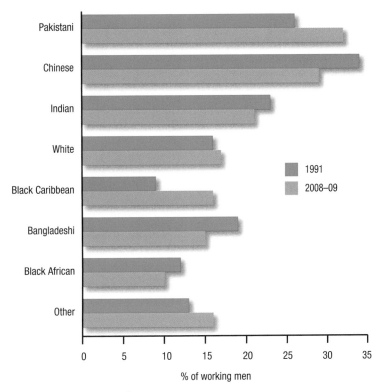

Figure 7.8 Self-employment by ethnic group ↑

of race, ethnic origin, religion or belief. Denying someone employment or promotion because they were Asian or Black or White would be direct discrimination.

Indirect discrimination occurs when everyone has to conform to the same practice that would deny a certain group opportunities. For example, if the police were required to wear only standard issue helmets it would indirectly discriminate against Sikhs whose culture requires them to wear a turban. (The police issue special turbans when this situation arises.)

Institutional discrimination occurs when an organisation's procedures and policies disadvantage people from ethnic minority backgrounds. It came to the fore in the Macpherson Report into the Metropolitan Police following the Stephen Lawrence Inquiry where it was defined as 'the collective failure of an organisation to provide an appropriate and professional service to people because of their colour, culture or ethnic origin. It can be seen or detected in the processes, attitudes and behaviour which amount to discrimination through unwitting prejudice, ignorance, thoughtlessness and racist stereotyping which disadvantage minority ethnic people.'

The impact of discrimination on income and living standards

Younger members of ethnic minority populations face fewer barriers than their parents faced. They are fluent in the local language, have a better grasp of UK social customs, have a wider social network and many have made good use of the education system.

However, there still appear to be barriers. For example, 24 per cent of Black African men have a degree level qualification which is significantly greater than the figure for White British males. Yet the unemployment rate for Black Africans is greater than the unemployment rate for Whites.

Race and religious discrimination contributes to the higher unemployment rates for many ethnic minority groups. Although the Race Relations Act was introduced in 1968, several studies over the years indicate that discrimination persists. The most recent *Home Office Citizenship Survey* published in 2005 reported that individuals from all ethnic minority groups were more likely than those from White ethnic groups to have been refused a job within the previous five years. A significant proportion of those believed they had been refused a job because of their race. Asians also felt their religion led to discrimination.

Blacks and Asians reported that race and colour were reasons for being refused a job on a high proportion of occasions. Blacks felt that their colour was twice as likely as Asians to be the reason for not getting a job, while it was 25 times more likely than a white person. Asians felt it was ten times more likely their race had cost them work than a white person, while a black person felt it was fourteen times more likely.

Figure 7.9 Ethnic minorities are underrepresented in the police force ↑

Minorities also felt they were denied promotion and advancement in their employment and careers as the result of race or colour discrimination. In addition, Asians felt their religion was a discriminatory factor. Muslims in particular, mainly Bangladeshis and Pakistanis, felt that since events in 2001, their religion was increasingly an issue that denied them jobs and promotion.

In Scotland minorities are under-represented in the police. There are 15,963 officers but only 118 are recorded as being black or Asian – there are 107 constables, eight sergeants, two inspectors and one superintendent. In the Lothian and Borders region, ethnic minority groups make up 2.5 per cent of the total population, but only 1.1 per cent of the force. In Strathclyde, minority groups represent 2.7 per cent of the population, but only 0.8 per cent of police officers. That amounts to about 70 police officers when there should be at least 150 to represent the community. The same applies to every police force area in Scotland, with the exception of Central Scotland Police.

In England and Wales there is a similar picture throughout the Criminal Justice System. Although they form 8 per cent of the population, ethnic minorities are under-represented in almost every area with the exception of the Criminal Prosecution Service and the Probation Service, but even here minorities are under-represented in promoted posts.

Table 7.5 **Success rate in getting a job interview (%)**

Group	%
White	60
Chinese	39
Asian	22
Black	13

Source: Commission for Racial Equality, 2005

Research undertaken by the Equality and Human Rights Commission (EHRC) attempted to see if people with the same qualifications but different ethnic backgrounds had similar success rates when applying for jobs. All applicants had different levels of difficulty in getting a job interview but, as Table 7.5 shows, Whites had far more success than any minority ethnic group. Blacks had by far the worst experience despite having equal or better qualifications and experience. This study demonstrates quite clearly the impact of discrimination in the job market as it exists today in the UK.

Activities

1   Draw up a table that shows the make-up of the ethnic minority population in Scotland and their relative risk of suffering poverty compared to Whites.

2   To what extent does each of the following factors contribute to income inequality for BME groups:

  ● cultural differences

  ● higher unemployment?

3   Explain each of the following terms:

  ● direct discrimination

  ● indirect discrimination

  ● institutional discrimination.

4   What evidence is there of discrimination reducing employment prospects for ethnic minority groups?

Racist harassment and racist attacks

Racism towards the minority communities has a major impact on their health, both physically and emotionally. In England and Wales recorded racist incidents are on the increase. Overall they rose by 7 per cent from 49,078 in 2002–03 to 52,694 in 2003–04. In Scotland, the total number of race crimes reported by the police to the Procurator Fiscal Service was 4314 in 2009–10. Since police began recording racist crimes in 2000 in Scotland, the number of incidents has risen by 75 per cent.

Part of this increase may be explained by a greater willingness on the part of victims to report these crimes. However, many organisations that represent minorities say that most incidents go unreported because the minorities have no confidence in the police. The clear-up rates are poor and with so few minorities on the force the communities do not feel it adequately represents them. A report by the Commission for Racial Equality Scotland stated, 'Verbal abuse ... was so much a part of everyday life that most people did not think of reporting it.'

A lot of these attacks are concentrated in poorer areas of cities where many disadvantaged minorities live. So, many who are forced by low income to live in such areas become the target of racist abuse and violence. The perpetrators are mostly youths. However, racism and racist violence spill over into all areas of our cities and affect ethnic minorities at all economic levels.

Racism can lead to physical violence. There were 52,694 racially aggravated crimes in 2003–04. Of these 14 per cent were for wounding and 11 per cent for assault. There were 22 homicides identified as having a 'known racial motivation'. Of these, twelve victims were White, four were Asian, three were Black and three were classed as 'other'. The rest were criminal damage (16%) and harassment, a high proportion of which takes place in or near the victims' home or property.

A major consequence is the emotional effect of having to face harassment in its many forms on a regular basis and the fear of living in a community in which unprovoked violence can erupt at any time. It is particularly stressful for someone to feel insecure in their own home and can lead to severe physical and emotional problems.

Research has found that the volume of racism is so great that it is sometimes difficult for individuals to isolate specific incidents. The worst offenders were found to be children and youths, and the main victims were children and youths in the minority communities. Most parents of the perpetrators were racists themselves and supported their offspring.

The racist attacks reduced the quality of life for the victims. Many victims changed their routines to avoid confrontation. Children were kept indoors or taken elsewhere to play. Adults left home early or returned late. In one case washing was hung to dry after dark. In some cases the victims gave up their home and moved.

The impact of income inequalities leads many ethnic minorities to live and work in areas where they face emotional and physical abuse, which has a detrimental effect on their wellbeing.

Race harassment and discrimination have an impact on health – both physical and mental. However, problems with mental health in particular go unreported. Research has shown that there are high levels of unreported psychological distress in Asian communities, and particularly among Asian women.

Mind, the mental health charity, states, 'It has been established and proven that Black people face discrimination in the fields of employment, housing and education. This means that like other minority ethnic groups, Black people are often denied access to, or given second-rate, opportunities. These conditions must have an impact on mental wellbeing.'

Physical abuse affects physical and psychological health. The fear of going out has an impact through lack of exercise. Notorious cases such as the deaths of Stephen Lawrence and of Anthony Walker are just the tip of the iceberg.

Following the London bombings in 2005, the level of racist attacks across England and Wales rose. Police in North Wales recorded 64 racist incidents following the suicide bombings compared to 20 the previous year. Racist and religious hate incidents rose to more than 800 in London within three weeks.

Government policies to reduce gender and ethnic inequalities

In recent years the Government has used a number of strategies to reduce gender and ethnic inequalities. The National Minimum Wage, Working Tax Credit and Child Tax Credit have been used to increase the income of the lowest wage earners. As many ethnic minority workers and women workers suffer from low-income employment these strategies have been of particular benefit.

Recent governments consider affordable child care as an important means of reducing the income gap. Child Tax Credit provides a working parent with up to 80 per cent of the cost of child care up to a maximum of £140 per week for one child and £240 for two or more children.

For women, poverty continues into old age because of interrupted working lives and years spent in part-time employment. Government policies have reduced the number of elderly living in poverty and the overwhelming majority of these are women. So Pension Credit has helped improve the income of women who retire with reduced pension entitlement. Winter Fuel Payment is also paid to most elderly women who have reached the qualifying age.

Equality Act 2010

There are also a number of Acts that try to eliminate gender inequalities. The Equality Act 2010 replaced nine major equality laws, including the Equal Pay Act 1970 and the Sex Discrimination Act 1975, and around 100 minor laws that existed previously. It covers gender, race, disability, religious belief, age and sexual orientation.

The Equality Act 2010 gives women (and men) a right to equal pay for equal work. The Act requires The Equality and Human Rights Commission

(EHRC, which was set up under the Equality Act 2006) to work towards the elimination of unlawful discrimination and promotion of equality.

The Commission can carry out inquiries into the extent and causes of pay differentials in particular areas of employment and can investigate an employer if it thinks that it has pay practices that are discriminatory. The Commission can help individuals to take legal action to enforce their right to equal pay. The Act gives employment tribunals the power to suggest how an employer can put things right for all their workers even if the person who complained no longer works for the company. For example, if a woman successfully complains that she has been unfairly treated and wins compensation, the employment tribunal can tell the employer how to change its practices so other women workers are treated fairly in future.

The Equality Act also says that companies with 250 or more workers have to publish information about the differences in men's and women's pay. The Government plans to do the same for public bodies with 150 or more workers.

Figure 7.10 Theresa May, Home Secretary and Minister for Women and Equality ↑

The Act also allows for positive discrimination. Job adverts can be aimed at different ethnic groups or women if the organisation does not have enough of that particular group. It can also train these groups to improve their chance of getting a better job with the organisation. The Act allows public organisations such as local councils to use their buying power to influence companies to include equality in the way they work. Public bodies spend £220 billion each year. They can use that power to influence companies that want their business to treat all their employees fairly.

The Equality Act requires all public bodies to think about treating people from different groups fairly and equally. For example, a local authority has to provide reasonable access to health care. If the local council finds that people in some areas cannot get reasonable access to a hospital because they have no car or it costs too much to park at the hospital, the council could provide a bus service.

The Equality Act 2010 requires health organisations to eliminate discrimination in the provision of health care and thereby reduce health inequalities for BME groups. For example, health care providers should be aware of the language needs of people living in their areas and provide health promotion in languages other than English. One authority provided smoking cessation programmes in Hindi, Urdu, Punjabi and Polish as well as English. Another example is the employment of multilingual speech therapists for BME toddlers with speech difficulties.

In Scotland, equality of provision is identified in the *Dimensions of Diversity Report*. It states, 'Many opportunities to improve the health of ethnic minorities lie in ensuring that services and initiatives are inclusive and are delivered through culturally sensitive means', which applies both to service planning and delivery. This means that when some minority ethnic groups have language difficulties accessing health care the NHS should provide information about services in appropriate languages and through cultural organisations that are in contact with minority groups such as mosques, community groups, etc. Bilingual workers or interpreters should be employed when talking to health professionals.

The same approach should also be used for health promotion and prevention campaigns. A recent Edinburgh study of health promotion initiatives related to cardiovascular disease and cancer prevention found that targeting intervention in Pakistani, Chinese and Indian communities brought about positive changes in knowledge and health.

Work and Families Act (2006)

The Work and Families Act (2006) entitles women to Statutory Maternity Pay (SMP) for 39 weeks. This is made up from 90 per cent of her salary for six weeks, and then £124.88 a week for another 33 weeks (2011). Some women can take a further 26 weeks of maternity leave, which is usually unpaid. Fathers can currently claim two weeks of Statutory Paternity Pay (SPP) at £124.88 a week or 90 per cent of their average weekly earnings, whichever is the least.

The Work and Families Act (2006) gives people the right to request flexible working hours in order to care for children under six, disabled children under eighteen and carers of disabled adults. It allows people to work while organising it around their caring role using such arrangements as flexi time, compressed hours where you work your hours over fewer days, job sharing, homeworking, etc. As women have a far greater role as carers this will help them more.

EMAG

The Ethnic Minority Advisory Group (EMAG) was set up to advise the Government about ways to reduce the higher rates of ethnic minority unemployment. It also advises the Government about ways to improve the education system so that members of minority ethnic groups do not leave school with limited hopes for their future. It tries to find ways to encourage more enterprise in minority ethnic communities and to encourage the Government to use its buying power to encourage greater diversity in the workplace among the organisations it buys services from.

EMAG is also trying to find practical ways to tackle the higher levels of unemployment among ethnic minority women. It aims to encourage moves towards equal pay and therefore improve their social mobility, encourage more flexible working arrangements, improve skills to provide access to work and tackle discrimination in getting work and getting promotion.

EHRC in Scotland

One important role of the EHRC is to monitor and report on pay divisions between the races and genders in unrepresentative public bodies. A major EHRC report of 2010, *How Fair is Britain?*, highlights the difficulties of disabled adults and minority ethnic women in finding work. Scotland's Commissioner Kaliani Lyle stated, 'What we have is a huge gap between our aspirations and our achievements. The Commission helpline takes calls every day from people experiencing real discrimination; women who are sacked because they are pregnant, people who face daily harassment because of their race and disability.' The report has been sent to every public body and Government department and this provides a wealth of evidence that organisations can use to develop strategies to avoid discriminatory practices.

In Scotland the Scottish Government, as a public body, is required to promote diversity and equal opportunities. It has a policy that all staff have to be treated equally irrespective of race or gender and to take steps to increase opportunities for women and ethnic minorities to work and gain promotion in the organisation.

Figure 7.11 Kaliani Lyle, Scotland's Equality and Human Rights Commissioner ↑

It looks to positively recruit staff from the minority ethnic communities and to actively encourage minorities and women to seek promotion throughout the organisation. Training opportunities are specifically targeted at minority ethnic people.

It has also provided around £2 million per year to support work around Scotland to encourage and promote race equality and opportunities such as:

- the Govanhill Law Centre has worked to promote race equality and promote good relations in some of the most deprived communities in Scotland
- Skillnet Edinburgh and the Bridges Programmes have worked with minority ethnic communities to reduce unemployment and under-employment
- a number of projects, such as Bridging the Gap, Dundee International Women's Centre, Amina – the Muslim Women's Resource Centre, and Saheliya – a Black and Ethnic Minority Women's Mental Health organisation, have worked to improve employment opportunities and empower minority ethnic women.

'Race for Health' is an organisation funded by the Department of Health in England and Wales to investigate and advance ways to improve health care provision for BME. It works with the NHS to promote ways to reduce race inequality in the treatment of diabetes, mental health, perinatal mortality and coronary heart disease and to advise on ways to implement race equality legislation as it applies to the NHS.

Success of government policies

It is clear that government programmes have had some success. Two groups that have seen significant reductions in poverty are lone parents and pensioners, which are overwhelmingly made up of women. For example, around 300,000 extra lone mothers have found employment and many have been lifted out of poverty in the last ten years.

However, women are still more likely to live in poverty than men and remain in poverty throughout their lives. Around 5 million women compared to 4 million men live in poverty. Many of these women are elderly because women continue to have worse pension entitlements and the government policy of means-tested benefits such as Pension Credit means that many women do not claim what they should.

As long as income inequalities remain, women will continue to be affected by health inequalities. Also, as women continue to live longer they will continue to have worse morbidity rates than men.

Despite government legislation and programmes such as 'Give Racism the Red Card' members of the minority ethnic community continue to face discrimination in employment. Some groups are using the education system to get access to higher-income employment but even here there is still evidence of inequality.

The Equality Act 2010 in the long term may deliver greater equality of opportunity for women and minority ethnic groups in employment, income and health. However,

the Equal Pay Act was passed in 1970, the Sex Discrimination Act in 1975 and the Race Relations Act in 1976, but we are still some way from equality in Scotland.

The riots in England, August 2011

The one consolation to be taken from the August riots which engulfed London and cities such as Manchester over three or four nights is that they were not a conflict between black people and the police (as happened in 2001 in Bradford). While it was the death of a black person in police custody which sparked off protest, what followed became an opportunity for people of all races to rampage the streets and empty the shops. Over 2000 people were later charged for their part in the riots, including murder charges against those who had run over and killed three Asian men in Birmingham. High youth unemployment, grim council estates, generations of toxic families living on welfare, and gang activity were all blamed. Yet Glasgow and Scotland – with some of the highest levels of deprivation – were spared the riots.

The Economist, in a September 2011 article, argued that race did play some part in the riots. While black people make up only 3 per cent of the UK population, CCTV placed on the Internet by the police displayed a significant number of black rioters. In contrast there was no disorder in districts with large Asian populations.

Educational attainment of African–Caribbean boys is low: only 56 per cent received five A*–C grades at GCSE compared to 74 per cent for all pupils. African–Caribbean boys are also more likely to be permanently excluded from school (10%) and to end up in prison as adults, making up 14 per cent of the prison population.

Concern has been expressed about the extent of family breakdown: 65 per cent of Black

Caribbean children grow up in a lone-parent family, and nine out of ten of these households are headed by women.

Timeline of the riots

From peaceful protest to country-wide riots.

- **4–6 August:** Mark Duggan was killed in Tottenham, London, after police stopped the car in which he was a passenger. Saturday's protest march sparked unrest and by the end of the night Tottenham was ablaze, with cars and shops set on fire and looters running free.
- **7–8 August:** More disturbances took place on Sunday night, but it was on Monday afternoon that they began to escalate. The violence spread first to Hackney, then to other parts of London, and then to major cities outside London.
- **9 August:** An extra 10,000 police meant the streets of London were quieter, but rioting and disorder took hold in Manchester, Birmingham, Nottingham, Wolverhampton and Liverpool.
- **10 August:** Looting and clashes with police continued into the early hours in many areas outside the capital. London remained calm. Three Asian men died when they were hit by a car in Birmingham – they were trying to protect their community. Meanwhile hundreds were arrested in the capital and elsewhere as the clean-up continued.

By the end of August over 2000 arrests had been made and 1400 jailed:

- 25 per cent of those charged over the riots had committed more than ten past offences.
- 75 per cent had a previous caution or conviction.
- 46 per cent were Black mixed race and 42 per cent were White.
- 60 per cent were claiming benefits.
- 90 per cent were male.

Figure 7.12 An iconic London bus set a blaze during the riots ↑

Activities

1. Which government policies, organisations or legislation have been introduced to help each of the following groups:
   - women
   - ethnic minorities?
2. Carry out an Internet search of the causes of the August 2011 riots in England.

Essay question

Critically assess the effectiveness of recent government policies in reducing inequalities for either ethnic minorities and/or women.